I BLAME TELEVISION

Essays on the Pop Culture that Raised, Ruined, and Enraptured Me

by Elizabeth Teets

Published by

Published by Read Furiously. First Edition - Trenton, NJ.

ISBN: 978-1-960869-25-8
LCCN: 2026935478

Memoir
Essays
LGBTQIA+
Television
Feminist Pop Culture

Cover Design by Matthew Revert.

For more information on *I Blame Television* or Read Furiously, please visit readfuriously.com. For inquiries, please contact info@readfuriously.com.

Read (v): The act of interpreting and understanding the written word.

Furiously (adv): To engage in an activity with passion and excitement.

**Read Often. Read Well.
Read Furiously**

To all the queers who have saved me time and time again.

To brave girls with big tits who burn hot and forge ahead at full speed.

To the beautiful clothes that held me together with their polyester threads.

And most of all to my mother who is going to read this book even though I told her not to.

This is a work of creative nonfiction. This book is built from the reruns of my life we call memories, recorded here in the form of personal essays. Like all reruns, a second or fifty-seventh rewatch feels different than the first time viewing. Some of the jokes hit at different spots then the original and some things feel a little different when seen through a new lens. Most of the names have been changed, except with the permission of those mentioned. Some event recollections have been abridged and some dialogue has been reconstructed.

TABLE OF CONTENTS

INTRODUCTION: ON PARODY

During the time I was working on this book, my friend Francesca came by my apartment in Hollywood on a late Saturday night. I made us air-popped popcorn and together we laid out on my California king bed that fills up half my tiny eighteen hundred a month studio and we browsed streaming services on my rose-colored Macbook Air looking at our film options. I stopped at one of my favorite films from childhood, *A Very Brady Sequel.*

"Isn't that a parody?" Francesca asked. Through her tone, which I was fluent in after years of friendship, I could understand her question was implying, *isn't this movie going to be dumb?*

"No," I replied confidently. I had seen *A Very Brady Sequel* many, many times. I knew every line and every joke, it having been one of the few VHS tapes I owned as a child.

"I've seen this a million times," I said confidently.

The next day I called my mom.

"Why didn't you tell me that *A Very Brady Sequel* was a parody?"

My mom laughed, "You just figured that out?"

Like most people who write humorous personal essay collections, I was a knowledge thirsty and astute child. I frequently listened in on and understood adult conversations so much that the school had to call my mother to apologize for the staff speaking about things they shouldn't in front of me, thinking the subject matter would go over my head, only to discover I absolutely did understand when I butted in on the conversation.

Despite this, I did not notice that *A Very Brady Sequel* is very much a parody. Like its predecessor *The Brady Bunch Movie* (which we did not own on VHS and I did not see until I was twenty-seven), the film uses retroactive continuity to place the Brady Bunch lore into the modern world of the 1990s. Throughout the film we get 1970s morality, lectures, white kid slang, and most importantly fashion, but with the sensibilities and, I would argue, seriousness of the 1990s.

The movie's humor comes from actors playing satirical versions of the original Bradys acting as if they are in a 1970s sitcom, while other characters they encounter act as if they are regular people in 1996. Much of the film's humor comes from making the Bradys the punch line as they are seemingly living in a fantasy world and unaware of how their thoughts and actions - considered outdated and most importantly naïve (or innocent) - are interpreted by those they encounter who live in the "real world."

To the rest of the inhabitants of the film's universe, the Bradys are all a little off, but they are unable to identify exactly why.

"I knew it was a comedy but I also thought it was an entirely serious film," I, a thirty-two-year old woman with a job and an expensive college degree, and who graduated high school a year early, explained to my now laughing mother on the other end of the phone.

What I meant was, when I watched the film regularly as a child, I knew the Bradys were in the 90s, like I was at the time. But I was unaware of the social and political subtext of the film's commentary, as well as the overt and frequent sexual innuendos. The movie has an entire sexual tension/incest plot between technically step-siblings Greg and Marcia that I somehow missed, thinking it was a regular teenage *will they-won't they* romance.

"Well, that's why I thought it was okay to show it to you because I knew you didn't get it," my mom continued, still very amused. "Then I started to hesitate because as you grew up you started getting the jokes and they were inappropriate for your age."

Although as an adult, I can see that most of the film script's intention is for the humor to be derived from parody, but it is also filled with classic sitcom humor, a simple and easy way to digest the type of comedy that I craved as a child.

The basic plot of *A Very Brady Sequel* centers around Trevor, a con man who poses as Carol Brady's deceased ex-husband Roy in order to become close to the Bradys so he can find an priceless ancient horse statue he believes to be somewhere in the Brady house. The gullible and naïve Bradys take Trevor's word that he is Roy despite his changed appearance (he tells them an elephant stepped on his face and he underwent plastic surgery) and welcome him to stay with them while they sort out what to do about Carol now having two living husbands. As "Roy" lives with the Bradys in order to look for the horse, he observes the Bradys' everyday life as if they are really in a simple 70s sitcom while working and attending school in the cynical 90s reality.

My mom was correct: as I grew up, I did start to get more of the jokes and some of the sexual innuendos and many of the more obvious over-the-top punch lines. But what I had never fully grasped until I rewatched the film in my thirties was that the world the Bradys were living in wasn't real. The Bradys lived in a created reality of the 70s sitcoms, where the rest of the world, the straight world, was in the film's present day of 1996.

In one scene, the Brady kids are on a plane and grow bored. In order to entertain themselves Greg pulls out a guitar and the Brady children do an entire song and dance number in the aisles while other passengers look on, annoyed at the absurdity of the situation and the Bradys' awful music. This is, of course, a more contemporary mockery of the wholesomeness of the real Brady Bunch music. However, my reading as a child viewer, who enjoyed the song and dance, was that the adults were being overdramatic because they were too uptight, boring, and not fun. I thought we were all in agreement that we should be laughing at the stuck-up adults, not the singing Bradys. And as someone who was recently on a red-eye flight with a teenage hockey team that couldn't stop doing "rounds of applause" every half hour, I am still giving serious side-eye to those airplane passengers who made fun of my Bradys' fun little music routine.

I always thought the joke was on the other people, not the protagonists. The Bradys had a nice life, they had good morals and values, cute clothes, and a nice loving, attractive family. Certainly, the joke was on the other guy. The composite characters, rolling their eyes at Marcia for brushing her hair too much or at Mr. and Mrs. Brady's loving relationship, were the ones we should mock, the ones we should feel sorry for because they didn't get it. They were so caught up in their own ways that they wouldn't let their guards down and just be happy.

As I watched the film as an adult, I related to the Bradys who were living in their own la la land as the rest of society mocked or felt confused by them. The entire setup felt pretty familiar, because I had been doing the same thing for years, living in my own reality and simply smiling and shining when someone pointed out the obvious, that I lived in my own optimistic world free of contemporary cynicism.

Because when you're queer, or a woman, or both you live in a world that does mock you and isn't built for you. One with different moralities, goals, and fashions. I am used to having sexual innuendos thrown at me from every angle and I brush them off just the same, just like the Bradys. I didn't notice the satire because it's not that different from how I navigate the world.

Parodies are often a divisive form of media. Many, like my friend Francesca as we tried to pick a movie that night, think parodies are stupid, lowbrow forms of comedy, an overexaggeration of the original source matter and nothing more. But they can also show us how interesting the original source matter was, what made it unique, original and creatively relevant. Parodies also show where the original falls short by deliberately exaggerating its flaws, outdated viewpoints, and weaknesses.

As I rewatched *A Very Brady Sequel* through my new adult eyes, I was reminded of another parody from my childhood, arguably the most talked about parody of the 1990s. Aqua's 1997 hit "Barbie Girl" was my first ever musical purchase. I had it on tape because everywhere in my hometown of

Corvallis, Oregon sold out of Aqua's album *Aquarium* on CD. My saintly mother had taken me to at least five stores to search for it. Begrudgingly, my mother was also nice enough to play *Aquarium*, which probably sounded like nails on a chalkboard to a woman who would much rather be listening to unreleased Prince tracks, on our rides to school in her blue Toyota almost every day for the remainder of the 90s.

In "Barbie Girl" Aqua members engage in a call and response as Barbie and Ken introduce the listener to their imagined world and lifestyle. Barbie introduces herself as a "blond bimbo girl in a fantasy world," a line Mattel detested so much they went on to try to sue the band for copyright infringement. The case was settled in Aqua's favor under parody protections on my birthday in 2002.[1]

As a child I didn't understand the nuance in the "Barbie Girl" lyrics which poke fun at the performed femininity and sexualization of the popular children's toy. Instead I longed to be a Barbie girl. Deep in my soul I felt the glamour in pink, I wanted to dress up and go to a party with my own fabulous Ken.

My favorite lines in "Barbie Girl" are both sung by René Dif as Ken in response to Lene Nyström as Barbie.

> *You're my doll, rock and roll, feel the glamour in pink. Kiss me here, touch me there, hanky-panky.*
> *Come jump in, bimbo friend, let us do it again. Hit the town, fool around, let's go party.*[2]

It is only in the second verse that Ken calls Barbie his bimbo friend, a derogatory word giving us the image of a blonde with big boobs and an empty head and ripe for mindless hairbrushing. And it is only after Barbie introduces herself to us as a bimbo. But the first part of the line, "feel the glamour in pink," seems to be directed at the audience. Telling us for a moment to stop thinking and drop our inhibitions and enter the Barbie world. Ken is not talking to Barbie, she is already familiar with the glamour. After all, she created it. Instead Ken is inviting us to join *her*. We can be like Barbie or the Bradys in a happy carefree dream, if we only accept the invitation.

The song's more advanced exploration of Barbie as a sex object and unrealistic symbol of femininity and vessel for misogyny was lost on my young ears. All I heard was a magical song about a Pepto-Bismol colored dream world that I wanted to be sucked into. "Barbie Girl" and *A Very Brady Sequel* both showed me a deliberately exaggerated femininity that I wanted to replicate. In Marcia and Barbie, I saw a life that was all hairbrushing and cute outfits and I wanted to build my own as fast as possible.

I have always had a heightened sense of my own femininity. I love platform heels, dangly earrings and big coats (useful for both fashion and fucking on top of). It's how I feel comfortable, how I feel most myself. And most importantly it is not for a man. As a queer woman coming from a somewhat religious Christian upbringing, I have always had my own sense of morality. And my entire life I have used humor to navigate the world when my own morals are at odds with society's. It's always been better to be a feminist or a queer with a joke and a wink, than to kill joy.

Much of this book is about my war with "the real world."

I am not supposed to feel comfortable in "the real world." I am a woman, I'm queer, I have knockers the size of traffic cones, I'm frivolous and overspend each month, I wear platform shoes I can barely walk in, my nail polish is always chipped, I eat most of my meals in bed, over half of my underwear have period stains, I don't laugh at men's jokes, I always forget to shave my big toe, I'm late to most things, I always pronounce the word "anecdote" wrong, I have a ton of credit card debt from my slutty little outfits, I spend half my day brushing my hair, and worst of all, I'm an unwavering optimist in a cynical society.

Much of this book is also about my time in the underground comedy scene. The furthest place from plastic, or pink, or 1970s floral prints. But I showed up as myself and never let the "realness" of that world suck me in too far.

When I entered the comedy scene at nineteen, I was a sheltered virgin with double Ds and hair made for endless brushing, confused by the bitterness of adult life. As I rewatched *A Very Brady Sequel*, the way the outside characters treat the Bradys felt hauntingly familiar to how I was and am treated in environments where I don't belong. When writing my first stand-up sets, I always preferred the punch lines to be on myself than other people. I saw the power in being the source of the joke rather than the cynical observer. It is better to be mocked for not fitting in than be the one mocking a third party for not conforming to a society I don't always respect. My own view of myself started to feel as though I am a satirical character living in a straight world.

Even my name, Elizabeth Teets, when I say it out loud sometimes feels like a joke. Like I was named something some horny male screenwriter made up to give to a silly girl with huge tits. When I say my name out loud, I feel like I should always be winking directly at the camera, making sure the camera gets the sexual innuendo.

As I worked on this essay collection intending to focus primarily on the pieces of pop culture that brought me joy, parodies began to show up more and more. The parody as a form critiques or mocks older social mores that are outdated. But in the inverted expectations, many viewers who already experience otherness can find themselves because we have always had expectations that are different. As a result, we sometimes identify with the bimbo friend and we find empowerment rather than mockery.

A Very Brady Sequel was also the film that introduced me to the word "gay." At the climax of the film Carol Brady is kidnapped and taken to Hawaii by Roy as they check into a hotel she remarks to the hotel desk clerk.

"I wish I could be gay again."[3]

The hotel clerk of course responds as if she means she wishes she could be a lesbian and not that she is wishful to return to her happy family.

"What does gay mean?" I asked my mother one day as I sat on the living room floor rewatching the VHS tape for possibly the thirtieth time, but likely in one of our earlier viewings before I understood too many jokes.

"It means happy." she said, "or it can mean boys kissing boys or girls kissing girls, but in the movie she means happy."

Carol continues to wish to return home by inadvertently doubling down on the joke.

"And I would be too if I were back with Marcia, and Jan

and Cindy."

It was the first time I heard that word and questioned its meaning. I am not the first queer person introduced to our identity in the form of a joke, but this one, for me, feels especially on the nose. For my first exposure, I heard it as a double entendre with an underlying smirk at a woman's naivety.

Throughout the film, every character the Bradys encounter knows that they are a little off, but they are unable to identify exactly why. This is a fundamental queer experience, of having the world seeing you as slightly off, but not always able to identify the source of the otherness.

But even with the darkly sinister undertones of both texts, Barbie and the Bradys shine brightly throughout their stories, narrowly escaping but each still prevails because they refuse to compromise their own values or leave their own world, the Bradys return home without their horse being stolen, Barbie escapes from sexual exploitation with her Ken, who adores her.

Many people find parodies stupid, low comedy. But for the people that love them, women, gays, obsessives with good taste, they remain cult classics. They make us squeal and captivate us, because we are in on the jokes, usually because to the straight world, we are the joke. And even if we see the cruel exaggeration it only makes us love it more. We feel the glamour in pink, we wish we could be gay again, we are usually the ones getting in trouble for singing and dancing on airplanes.

I think it's funny now that I didn't get it. Maybe we should blame my mom for sheltering me and it taking so long to see that the movie was a parody, or maybe she is just an excellent parent keeping the real world at bay. I'm glad I lived in my own little world for so long.

I didn't know I was watching a joke because to me the world was real. And even now, it still is. And as the world gets more and more absurd, I embrace these parts of myself that are blindly unaware when the world is making fun of optimism, femininity, queerness, or hopefulness. Because as Jan Brady teaches us, you can't meet George Tropicana Glass unless you have the imagination to make him up.

But it is the same sense of otherness that allows us to create the jokes, because we are who holds the power. We laugh away, smiling, while the normal folks stand around confused. To this day when someone makes a joke at my expense, I don't always immediately get it. I don't always hear backhanded compliments, instead I take them at face value.

I am a somewhat naturally confident person when I move through the world. I cannot help but think that a lot of that comes from the pop culture I enjoy most. Parodies show us the most confident characters because they are utterly unaware anything they are doing is socially wrong. There is power in not letting shit get you down and not letting the bitterness and cruelty of others break the joy we have created for ourselves. In the many times I've heard "nice outfit" I've always smiled and said thank you.

All my favorite female characters Elle Woods, Cher Horowitz in *Clueless*, Lisa Simpson, or Fran Fine are laughed at. Sometimes they notice but then they quickly move on. Because they are sure of themselves and sure of their decisions on how to move through a world that is not made for them. We laugh at the heightened characters parodies or comedies show us, because they seem out of touch. But for many of us who also live in a world not made for us, we see these unapologetic characters as the most authentic.

As I was writing this collection I came across a viral video of three little girls, probably in early elementary school, dancing to Chappell Roan's "Pink Pony Club" while they held each other's hands in a circle. They sang to each other fully in the moment unaware of the camera capturing their bliss. While I saw a tender moment of girlhood and friendship, many of the comments on the video were quick to sarcastically mention that they don't know they are dancing to a song about a strip club. It's true, they probably don't; to little girls when they hear the lyrics, to them they are really at the pink pony club, a magical place "where boys and girls can all be queens every single day."[4] I am happy for those of them taking the lyrics literally, they get a song about a sparkly paradise to play and be free. I hope they take as long to learn the true meaning as it took for me to get the sexual implications of "Barbie Girl," so they can live in their dream world a little bit longer, and I hope when they learn the meaning they still want to go to the "Pink Pony Club," but for different reasons.

I love the world that parodies create because innocence can still live. I love the characters in parodies because they don't know how to self-correct, something I still cannot do. I don't know how to feel shame when I don't think something is shameful. I don't know how to fall in line, I don't know how to feel pessimistic as a hobby, I don't know how to feel comfortable in a polo or sensible shoes. I often feel like I wake up in my pristinely perfect world I've created for myself and I wouldn't notice the man behind the curtain unless you pointed him out.

I still sometimes want to live with the Bradys, or at the Pink Pony Club, or in the Barbie World and this book is for everyone else who has felt that they needed a different world, but had to make do in this one because it's all we have.

We may have to live in the real world but we can at least make our own houses within them. We can carve out our own space for glamour and rooms without shame or cynicism.

So welcome to my Dream House, things might feel a little off here.

Elizabeth Teets

BECAUSE MY MOM CAN'T CRY

Every Saturday there was a different woman in our house crying her eyes out on our couch. The drugstore makeup streamed down their blotchy faces, quickly wiped off with their sleeves. Soon, and without warning, the crying turned into wailing and then harmonized in unison with my mother's cackles, as she had been laughing the entire time.

My mother has never cried during a movie. Her coworkers, fellow nonclinical workers at a child psychiatric outpatient program, were shocked upon this discovery. *Not even My Girl? Not even Forrest Gump? What about Steel Magnolias?* Although tough and unshakable to me, to them a single mother in her mid-twenties probably seemed like a nut with a tough exterior that could be cracked with some gentle prodding. They knew my mother to be kind and empathetic, so they all bet they could find the movie that would make her cry.

If they would have asked me, I would have told them to save their money. How the situation unfolded and how the movie nights started happening, I do not know. I am not even sure if it was an organized bet or what the rules of the game were, but I assume they were along the lines of: if you could get her to shed a tear, the victor won some pooled money or a free lunch at Applebee's or some other 1990s chain restaurant. Despite working at a mental health facility for children, which I had visited many times throughout my childhood, the area my mom worked in was a typical late 1990s office with Koosh balls and Rubik's Cubes on desks while Third Eye Blind played softly on the radio.

The bet went on for a few weeks. Coworkers my mom considered friends were entering our living room, trying to battle the monster of my mother's emotional depth by showing us the most depressing moments in all of cinema history on our nineteen-inch Panasonic. This was usually accompanied by the sounds of whichever woman had brought what they were sure was the winning VHS tape, sobbing loudly into our Saturday nights.

I don't remember almost any of the movies we watched. My memory instead is filled with what I was obsessed with at the time. I was in the first grade, and at that time my viewing was limited to *Sabrina the Teenage Witch*, *The Simpsons* (religiously as long as I closed my eyes during *The Itchy & Scratchy Show* per my mom's rules), and the Foodsaver infomercial (an hours-long odyssey of advertising I have watched to completion enough times to quote). All of these superb viewing experiences were accompanied by my mom's voice telling me I was too close to the TV and would hurt my eyes.

The new sad movies being brought into my world did not have magic, jokes, or even kitchen appliances available at a special price if you call within the next fifteen minutes. They did not hold my interest. However, watching my mother react to them did. I remember her starting each one with a slight smirk on her face that only got wider as one of her co-workers broke down, and she remained completely composed until the credits rolled.

The worst of the sobbing sessions were from my mom's friend Rosey. She sat with a tissue held up to her red, puffy face while watching the movie she had chosen in an attempt to crack the beast. My mom looked at her from across the couch and laughed at her best friend as Rosey cried more, choking out, "It's sad!" in between sobs.

Watching this unfold, I wondered if my mommy was mean. Like the girls at my school, she was laughing while her friend cried. Like kids on the playground laughing when my long hair got stuck in the chains from the swing sets.

My mom has always had what, as a kid, I thought was a slight icy layer. As a child, I assumed it was because she became a single parent at nineteen, and she played the role of both mother and father. I now know that isn't cold at all; she is just what you would call a *bad bitch*. As an adult, anybody I've ever had over to meet has been terrified of her, but at the same time remarked she was very nice.

I love my mom. I want to put her in my mouth like a cotton ball and swallow her whole so I can carry her around in my gut. Every nightmare I ever wake up from screaming involves her death. I dream about her dying so often, and I have called her so many times after waking up from a bad dream that she recently jokingly asked me to "please stop trying to kill her off." But I can't imagine anything scarier than her not being with me. I love her when she is in a good mood, and she calls me by my special only-for-her nickname "buddy," and we chat on the phone about stupid stuff. I love it when she is distracted or tired and prickly, and she tries to get me off the phone as quickly as possible because I know she will feel bad and then call back within twelve hours, but probably less.

When I had my first boyfriend over, she gave him a beer

first before grilling him with questions about the many unkind ways he had been treating me and his tendencies to cancel on me at the last minute. He sweated through his shirt-the beer did not, in fact, take the edge off. Nothing has made me feel safer knowing she was in my court; I like that my mom has an edge.

My mom's particular edge and grit were especially noticeable to me that night, in her laugh while Rosey cried. The plot of the movie that quickly brought Rosey to hysterical tears was the only one whose plot I slightly remembered. In the movie, a bunch of strangers die on a bus and then haunt a baby until he grows into an adult so they can take over his body. At one point, the ghosts leave the kid when he is in elementary school, and the kid is sad because the ghosts were his secret friends. Rosey sobbed through the duration of this ghost and kid saga while my mother, the dragon lady, sat in cold icy silence peppered with a few smirks and tiny giggles.

At the time, I was known to cry regularly in my grade school whimsically at many things that came across my television. Most notably, daily at the "Save the Children" commercials because I could not fathom that I had a life so much more wonderful than these kids in Africa. I had not yet realized I was living in a trailer park, eating free school lunches, being raised by a single mother. The level of gratitude I had for my small life is something I will search for in therapy for years to come. But even I could not fathom why Rosey found this kid-can-see-ghosts movie so sad. But I assumed it was really for adults, and I would get it someday. I knew I would cry like Rosey. I didn't want to be like my mom. I didn't want to be a dragon lady.

I now know my mom's exterior grit came from her need to keep our lives together, and she did; she always had that shit on lock. She not only had to take on the role of both parents but also acted as the sole breadwinner. On top of that, she was struggling with undiagnosed celiac disease. Although my mother naturally ran hot, bread, an unknown enemy, fueled her anger at whatever situation pushed her over the edge. Whenever I *did* see her cry, it was generally within the context of her being angry. I never really saw her shed tears unless her face was also red hot. These angry tears were only for me. Since I was the only one that could really make her angry, I was the only one that could make her cry. Because of this, I often felt like I was walking on eggshells around her, not yet understanding female rage and its multitudes. While her co-workers were trying to break the beast, I was trying not to awaken it. Since moving to a gluten-free diet, I have watched the woman who I once felt was a ticking time bomb turn into someone who only raises her voice when she feels it is absolutely necessary. In a way, this makes her more terrifying, to the point it's kind of inspiring.

When I asked my mom why she never cried at movies, her answer surprised me. "I feel sad inside," she said. "The only movie that has ever made me want to cry is *Hope Floats*. It has a lot of mother-daughter things that made me really sad." To me, this made sense; I always knew that I was the center of my mother's world.

One night when I was in my late twenties, I scrolled through the HBO app, looking for something to stream. I saw a cover I instantly recognized as the "sad-ghost-kid" movie. I was shocked to discover the movie that had made me think my mother was heartless, *Heart and Souls...* was a comedy and in my HBO Max queue under "Uplifting."

I had to watch it immediately. Maybe it was categorized wrong? Maybe there was one really sad scene? After watching the movie, *Heart and Souls*, all I discovered is that Rosey cried hysterically at maybe the cheesiest movie ever made. *Heart and Souls* is charming, I guess, but mostly in an overly earnest way that is off-putting.

It did not make me laugh or cry; it mostly made me confused. It is a fine, but rather bland, film. The film is a heartwarming depiction of a possible afterlife, I suppose, but I found it gimmicky and nowhere near the punch to the gut I was expecting. My mom's lack of sad tears no longer seemed so absurd. But for so long, my mom's not crying at movies had become part of her identity to me. I could not get the image of her seeing the "sad ghost kid movie" and being so unmoved while Rosey could barely breathe through her snot.

The only thing in the media, be it movies or music or television, that has ever gotten my mother truly emotional is anything having to do with mother-daughter relationships. Having been a young single mom, or more accurately, being my mom at any age or point in history, is a big part of her identity and the root of all her biggest fears. The movies she loves aren't movies where mothers and daughters are the best of friends, but the ones where there is conflict and they talk and scream and cry and yell and, most importantly, get through it.

I never considered that the fascination my mother has for mother-daughter dynamics was an act of love. Our relationship is complicated, as most mother-daughter relationships are. But I feel deeply fortunate to have a mother who is as obsessed with our dynamic as I am and interested in learning how to communicate while obsessively studying examples in the media.

It is one of these examples of a mother-daughter relationship that my mother was and is so obsessed with that made me become a stand-up comedian. For the film dorks in the back, I am, of course, talking about the Nora Ephron directorial debut *This is My Life*.

Growing up, we had a VHS copy of *This is My Life*, which, due to not having more than four channels for the bulk of my elementary school years, I have seen hundreds of times. To my mother, *This Is My Life* is a movie about a young single mom trying to balance motherhood and career. To me, *This is My Life* is a movie about a woman becoming a stand-up comedian.

In reality, of course, it is both movies. Dottie Ingels, a young single mother of two daughters, Erica and Opal, comes into an inheritance when her aunt dies, and with the money takes her children to New York City to further her stand-up career.

I think my mother probably related to Erica, the sensible daughter, and saw Dottie as a version of the mother she didn't want to be. She saw Dottie as the villain of the movie, one she could easily become, a self-absorbed, ambitious mother who leaves her children lonely. She probably would have never guessed I would grow up to be a Dottie. Someone should have told her what happens when you expose your child to too much Nora Ephron at a young age.

In one of my early sets, when I first talked about my mom

on stage, I thought about *This Is My Life*. A large point of conflict in the film is using your own life for material. Whose story belongs to whom? At one point, Dottie points out the obvious: "It's just that our lives are all tangled up together." In this life, I am Dottie; my mother is Erica. And our lives are tangled up all together. "Why are you sharing things that are my life?" is a big part of the contention for Erica after she is upset when her mom talks about her during a late night appearance.[1] It is interesting to me, now that sharing too much is a big point of contention for my mother. I became a comedian talking about our intimate lives for all to see. My mother hates it when I talk about her on stage. The same is true with my writing, and she will probably at first not be excited about this book nor this essay.

She also really likes it.

I often wonder what it's like to be my mom. To have the love of your life (me) talk about you, make fun of you. Does she know the obsession goes both ways? That I create to understand her, to remember her, to get to know her.

My mom doesn't cry often, but she laughs a lot. At anything and everything.

"Oh my god, you are going to die laughing" is her most used sentence. She makes other people laugh. She is my favorite person to make laugh. It is my greatest privilege. It is a gift that our lives are all tangled up together, that our memories are floating together, some the same, some wildly different, but a tangled web of both our lives. Until I have another bad dream and accidentally kill her off again. I cannot be responsible for my subconscious.

Eventually the women stopped coming to our house

on Saturdays. No one won the bet. My mom will never cry at movies; she only really cries at me on the rare occasion, gets mad and fights with me over something stupid and unimportant. Probably because I shared too much about my life, about our life. Maybe we will fight because of this book, because our lives are tangled up all together. Both of us not knowing whose story belongs to whom.

FIGHTING FOR KATHLEEN

The rules of the assignment were simple. Pick any figure important to US history, write a research paper, do a five-minute presentation to the class in costume, and make a cutout of their bust to put on the wall. It would count as our final for AP US History.

After class I, along with the other students, lined up in front of Mr. Stephen's desk to give him the name of my chosen historical figure. The Sgt. Pepper's Report was Mr. Stephen's own invention. By this time, we had already studied for and taken the AP US History exam. In most of our AP classes, we were allowed to mostly dick around until the end of the school year. Mr. Stephen, like most of my middle-aged, white male high school teachers, was an avid lover of The Beatles. He did the project every year so he could recreate the *Sgt. Pepper's Lonely Hearts Club Band* album cover on his classroom wall, only this time with our favorite historical figures, which is why our cutouts were needed. Mr. Stephen supplied his own very expensive, custom-made cutouts of George, Paul, John, and Ringo for the wall.

For our junior year (which was also my last year of high school since I graduated early), we had listened as Mr. Stephen taught us about the various villains in US history: Confederate soldiers, Nazis, and slave traders, but there was no one he hated more than Yoko Ono. She was his usual punch line for every joke involving a bad guy. No one could ever be as villainous as Yoko.

We all knew the project was coming; it was the crème de la crème of high school history projects. Our senior friends had all done it and thought it was a super fun assignment, a chance to dress up and be creative and talk about what parts of history we liked. We were given free rein to pick whomever we liked, no matter if they were in our textbook or not.

Seniors always recommended Mr. Stephen to upcoming juniors when it came time to choose classes. Mr. Stephen was one of the teachers that was considered cool. He played music in the classroom, mostly classic rock mixed with the occasional jazz track or Johnny Cash, so he could lecture us on the importance of having an "eclectic" taste. He talked in a loud, expressive voice and was fond of using an air horn during his lectures. He suggested the *Animaniacs* songs on presidents and the fifty states as an easy way to remember crucial information for the AP test. He talked endlessly about his fraternity brothers and told countless stories that, at the time, we didn't realize weren't actually funny; however, we were still too young to know the difference between a white male teacher with confidence and true comedic chops. He referred to Obama's inauguration speech, which aired live at the same time as our class, as a "rude interruption by our forty-fourth President."

Before I enrolled in AP US History, I had known I was going to do my Sgt. Pepper's report on Kathleen Hanna. Being from the Pacific Northwest and a teenager who loved punk rock, I loved Bikini Kill. I planned an exciting presentation on the grandmother of third-wave feminism. Kathleen Hanna was my personal hero: both a punk legend and feminist icon, and one part of a celebrity power couple with a Beastie Boy. Mostly, I was excited to show my classmates that feminism was punk and cool.

I first discovered Bikini Kill through my teenage Green Day obsession. I got the research gene from my father, so anything I loved had to be explored thoroughly. These studies led me to the East Bay punk scene. I spent my babysitting money buying albums from bands like Operation Ivy and Crimpshrine, and through Crimpshrine, the writings of Aaron Cometbus, who quickly became my favorite writer. Kathleen is featured on Green Day's *American Idiot* album and sings the opening for the song "Letterbomb." After seeing her name in the album notes, I bought my first Bikini Kill record and from there I found Kathleen and her unpretentious gateway to feminism that had started my early awakening.

In line for Mr. Stephen's sign-up sheet, I heard my classmates pick their historical figures. He hooted and hollered upon hearing each student's pick. Students chose everyone from Sacagawea to the GoJo Hands infomercial guy, who had "changed commercials in the US," so therefore counted as historic.

"Who's it gonna be, Elizabeth?" Mr. Stephen asked me when I arrived.

"Kathleen Hanna," I said.

"Come again?" asked Mr. Stephen.

"Kathleen Hanna, the founder of the Riot Grrrl movement. The singer from Bikini Kill."

"Who?"

"You know, Bikini Kill, the punk band," I said, expecting him to know.

"The person has to be important to US history and have changed it in some way."

I was confused. I considered Kathleen Hanna as important to American history and culture as someone like Hemingway or Andrew Jackson. Since I was on track to graduate from high school early, I had been taking women's studies courses online through the community college to gain extra credits. Kaltheen had appeared in nearly all of my textbooks. I knew she was important to US history. But my confusion stemmed from his initial rejection of my choice: he was letting former SNL cast members, who were not even Gilda Radner, count as significant to American history.

"But Kathleen Hanna is a feminist icon," I said exasperatedly into my fifty-something, white, probably Republican schoolteacher's face.

"I listen to loads of punk music*, and I've never heard of her," he said back to me, as if that settled it.

It was the most I had ever been enraged after hearing a *no*. As a sixteen-year-old girl, I had heard many, many *nos* at this point, and I was used to them. *No* to dyeing my hair blue. *No* to dropping out to go to cooking school by day and becoming an art historian by night. *No* to rejecting my uncle's hugs when he creeped me out, because it was impolite. *No* to following My Chemical Romance on tour. *No* to bisexuality, which didn't exist.

But this *no* was different. This *no* was wrong. It was an injustice.

---

*I think he had the first Beastie Boys album and probably some Fall Out Boy.

I was lucky enough to go to a high school with many creative teachers. I was, however, taught US history by a straight white man. That's the one subject that they shouldn't be allowed to touch anymore. They already have done enough damage.

~

In 1989, Kathleen Hanna formed the punk band Bikini Kill along with guitarist Billy Karren, bassist Kathi Wilcox, and drummer Tobi Vail. Kathleen had come to music after her work as a spoken word artist. Bikini Kill, displeased with the hyper-masculine environment of punk shows, encouraged girls to come to the front in order to change the power dynamics of the room and keep women audience members safe-from both the violence of the mosh pit and any general creeps. The band, along with their fanzine, came to spearhead the Riot Grrrl movement, which combined punk rock with feminist politics. The Riot Grrrl movement is often cited as the start of the third-wave of feminism.

The first time I heard a Bikini Kill record, as a thirteen-year-old alone in my room, hiding from the man who was unfortunately my stepdad at the time, I felt like my world had burst open. I was intoxicated by Kathleen's voice as she screamed at the top of her lungs. I wanted to scream too.

I fell in love with Kathleen and her cool clothes, hanging on to her every genius word. I loved listening to her valley girl accent and was thrilled to hear someone sound so smart using words like I did. I kept pictures of her in my notebook, excited to see someone punk and feminist wearing colorblock skirts and pencil-cut dresses just like I did.

In many ways Kathleen was my feminist older sister, taking what she had read in more difficult feminist theory books and filtering it through a punk-rock lens so teenagers like me could understand.

It was through Kathleen that I understood that I could feel upset about the emotional violence I had experienced at home and not carry it with me, as if it was just "it is what it is." Someone felt as much rage as I did. Someone else was sick of being told they didn't have control of their own body. Someone else had also grown up afraid of the men in their own house.* Someone else had been told to be nice to the men who leered at us, because you must always respect your elders.

I listened to "Rebel Girl" on repeat. Kathleen was probably singing about someone she knew, but I listened to it as if I was singing it to her.

Rebel girl, you are the queen of my world.[1]

I went back to Mr. Stephen that afternoon and demanded he allow me to do the assignment on her, showing him my Women Studies 101 textbook.

It enraged me that just because something was made for women, and women alone, it became something with no value. I still wasn't ready to fight for myself in any real way, but I wasn't going to let any man tell me my hero wasn't important.

No one could tell me I couldn't write about her. I couldn't scream for myself. I couldn't make demands for myself yet, but I could make demands for her.

---

*Luckily by the time I reached high school I had a gem of a man for a stepdad. Love you Ricky.

~

An important thing to know about me even as you are reading this essay collection and consistently laughing, because these jokes just fly onto the page like nothing is that I didn't start out very good at stand-up comedy. I am much better now, but for many, many years I was cringeworthy bad on stage. I wasn't confident and couldn't connect with the audience the way I can now. The other important thing to know about me is that I knew this, and I continued to do it anyway.

Being bad at something is a privilege usually given to white men. Being bad at something and then being nurtured and groomed into a mediocrity we decide to call greatness seems to be a particularly white male experience. Women and minorities are generally not provided this luxury.

If it were not for Bikini Kill and for Kathleen, I never would have had the nerve to be bad at something and do it anyway. Bikini Kill didn't know how to be a band. They famously couldn't play their instruments. When anyone dared to point it out, they would laugh.

Tobi Vail laughs when she is asked about it in the Kathleen-centered documentary *The Punk Singer*.

People would say, "You can't play your instruments," and we would say, "And?"[2]

As a teen I was dumbfounded by the gumption. I felt like I could never do anything right, and they were okay being public and on stage in front of people doing everything very wrong.

I took Riot Grrrl philosophy with me into my first years of comedy. I was okay if I wasn't technically the best, as long as I came to the stage with something worthwhile to say. Which was more than I could say for the majority of my male peers.

I also got better at stand-up. Slowly and through hard work and with little support, but through my own persistence. I didn't care if my jokes always landed with every audience. I didn't care if a group full of boys didn't laugh. If a guy after a show told me I wasn't funny, I wouldn't even give him the time of day - who cared what he thought? I wanted the girls to laugh. I would see girls on dates with losers and think: *they are who I want to perform for.* I wish it was only us.

Kathleen did it all, and she was bad at it. In the same way, the boys are bad at it. But also not in the same way because men never think they are bad at anything, just "new" to it.

Not long after starting stand-up, I became a writer for a punk rock satire site. Writing satire is something that has always come relatively easy for me. I enjoy its formulaic structure and think of it more as filling in the blank. I was thrilled to finally have a part of my comedy path that came easily.

I was added to the satire site's online pitch group and found that it contained over two hundred writers, eleven of them women.

Not long after I began writing for the site, a pitch caught my eye.

"Hot Tips to Get You Bikini Kill Ready This Summer"[3]

I laughed out loud when I saw the headline. I was delighted to see the writer was one of my friends. *Yay! Another Kathleen lover,* I thought.

To my surprise the pitch was rejected by the (all-male) editorial team despite positive feedback from many of the other writers. Other similar jokes were rejected, including one about Kathleen herself from another woman whose writing I admired.

Finally someone asked the site's founder and editor-in-chief. "I don't know who that is, so it's not right for the site," he finally responded.

Again I was angry. I felt like a sixteen-year-old girl again. It was one thing to be enraged at a middle school or high school teacher who didn't know punk rock history and another at someone who ran a punk rock satire site. If you don't have a penis, it's almost like you don't exist.

Here it was happening again. This time from people who were supposed to understand punk rock enough in order to satirize it professionally. It was absurd.

Once again I had to fight for Kathleen's spot in punk history (and the satirizing of the culture), only this time I had ten co-fighters. First, we schooled our editor on the history of the Riot Grrrl movement, then we started a group chat where we could talk about his ignorance. Eventually it expanded into other topics, and in a way my own Riot Grrrl community was born.

But the problems didn't end after the Kathleen headlines were finally published. I asked over and over again for the editor to book me on the stand-up show that the website sponsored. I was told over and over the show was full. Each month it was always full of men who did not write for the website. There is no room for me, their highest clicked writer. By that time, I had gotten pretty good at being on stage.

Eventually I stopped asking and stopped writing for the site. Not as revenge - I simply outgrew it and didn't feel that I needed to fight for the approval from mediocrity. I got another satire writing job that paid better for a site that was a passion project of a former child star. The headlines I wrote paid off the bulk of my remaining student loans.

The day I gave my Sgt. Pepper's Project presentation, I wore my Kathleen costume to school all day. I introduced Riot Grrrl and Bikini Kill and everything I loved to my classmates.

In order to appease Mr. Stephen, I made sure to mention that it was Kathleen who had spray-painted "smells like Teen Spirit" on Kurt Cobain's bedroom wall.

Mr. Stephen gave me an A.

At the end of my presentation, he played all of *Nevermind* like it was Kathleen's greatest achievement. As if.

I met Tomy on the first day of sixth grade at our painfully suburban Vancouver, Washington middle school. Like many friendships of adolescence, we were friends, and then we were not, and then we were again, all depending on the day. Our petty arguments entertained us (many about where we were on each other's Myspace top friends), and created enough drama to fill all our three years of middle school and my three years of high school.*

At first, much of our daily theatrics were performed through secret three-way calls. Throughout middle school, Tomy and I would fight (over nail polish or Fall Out Boy or whatever new sweaters our moms bought us) and then, at least once a week, declare we were no longer speaking to each other. That was the set up. It was after that our game would begin. Over and over we terrorized our mutual friends by insisting they call one of us, while the other would also be secretly on the line. Despite all of our mutuals knowing this little dance, somehow we still always managed to charm a third wheel into our betrayal against the other.

The magic of a three-way call went something like this: I would be mad at Tomy so I would call a mutual friend of ours and insist she call him.

"Kaitlin, call Tomy but DO NOT tell him I'm listening,

*I graduated early for no other reason than to say I did.

I bet he will say something about me." Then whatever Kaitlin or Becky we had looped in, would accept the challenge and call Tomy as if it was just a regular chat with a casual friend. Tomy would pick up the call and purr casually into the receiver "Kaitlin, my love, how are you?" and pretend to not know I was definitely on the line as he spoke with her, probably while bedazzling a denim vest.

Meanwhile I would be silently listening in, as I lay in my teenage bedroom a few streets away under Green Day posters and pictures of Gwen Stefani pulled out from magazines. Tomy would then tell our unsuspecting third wheel that he was not speaking to "that bitch" at the moment, and was looking for new friends to hang out with. Then we would get to the good stuff. "You know she swore me to secrecy but I'm going to tell you because *you're my real friend Kaitlin**...," Tomy would say before he spilled one of my deepest secrets.

We would take turns doing this, each time one of us sitting silently, before dramatically revealing ourselves to having been on the call the whole time and claiming betrayal. *Et tu, Tomy? Et tu, Elizabeth?* Then we would make up, because the VMAs were about to be on, and we needed to discuss. I realize now how queer we were, and how unsubtle we were about it. When I think about those calls now, all I see is a perfect dance, a true love I will never get back.

The night after one of Tomy's fifteenth birthday parties[†] where he had officially come out as gay to the group of our gathered classmates, he called me up, clearly in a mood.

---

* Or Becky or Katie or Maddy. Wait, who am I talking to again?
[†] I went to at least two others.

"Whats wrong? Spill?" I demanded, thirsty for his thoughts. He told me was upset that his coming out wasn't a "bigger deal." I reminded him everyone knew he was dating a guy named Romeo, so what did he expect? What's gayer than a boyfriend? Romeo, despite having a similar build, looked like the reverse version of Tomy. He had bleached, neck length, overly flat ironed hair that was parted all the way to the side that contrasted Tomy's teased, black box dyed, also overly flat-ironed tresses. Romeo lived in Canada and had come down for the party, which was good because he looked like a Myspace scene kid that only existed on the internet. So it was nice to see he was a real suburban teenager and not a Catfish.

"I thought I would get more out of it," Tomy said, absolute in his opinion, that his coming out should have held more weight. I tried not to roll my eyes.

Tomy's gayness was obvious and had been for a long time. Tomy wore eyeliner to school, hung out with primarily girls, and wore his tight skinny grey jeans low under the puppy fat of his round belly. At our school of mostly white wealthy students, he stuck out as a plus-sized Latina, and so he did what any queer person learns to do: he stood out.

Tomy was always hoping to get more out of everything. Didn't matter if it was at one of the pop rock concerts we would go to or if we dragged ourselves to Portland for a night out dancing at the Escape, he never was ready for anything to end. And honestly it's a trait we share - we savored every experience for all it's worth.

In hindsight, it's not surprising he was the first one to die. *I should have known*, I thought a few days after it happened, sitting in my car letting the tears stream down my face. He left the biggest fucking hole, caused the most drama and pain, because he was everyone's favorite. A fucking queen to the end, always sticking out from the rest of the crowd. Even though his name had to be original, his Myspace profile explained to all those who didn't get it: "My name is Tomy but I spell it with only one M, I don't get it either!"

As a teen, I constantly needed his approval even though I would sometimes be faced with a bully who knew too much about me rather than someone whom I considered my best friend. It didn't matter how he treated me; I needed another queer person around, someone who got it even if I myself didn't get it yet. He was my chosen family, even if I couldn't always trust him, even if he wasn't always nice. He was the love of my teenage life.

I do not remember how I learned that Tomy had died. I should remember, it troubles me, but the exact moment is gone. If I'm being honest, I probably can't access it because the wound is too big, a trauma so big my brian has blacked out the pain. So the how of it has been shed from my memory - honestly, it was likely a Facebook post. I do remember I immediately called my mom and told her. She asked me if I was okay and I told her that I hadn't talked to him in a long time. I was twenty-five and, honestly, we had not been friends for quite a while. I sat and tried to cry and thought about the backs of his hands touching mine.

We hadn't spoken recently, but he had tagged me in something on Facebook not long before. Something music related that he knew I would like. Posting a link on my Facebook wall with the words "OMG Elizabeth." This was a big deal - Tomy never reached out to anyone he didn't feel was worth his time and cool. It felt good to know he was watching me on the internet. I was living in Portland, Oregon at the time, and he was still in the suburbs we grew up in across the river in Vancouver, Washington. He wasn't far from me, but by that point it was like he was a world away, but if either of us wanted each other, we were really only twenty minutes apart.

When we were in high school, which was right next to the middle school where we had met, I wanted him to want me around so badly. He was the first man other than my father whose attention I pined for. Sometimes I actually wanted him around too, but mostly I just wanted him to want me. I longed for the thrill of being his desired company. He rarely responded to my texts, but we were together a lot during school and after. I know with certainty that he loved me, but he also had a way of making it clear my company, although consistent, was not his first choice.

Despite this, we spent plenty of time together. His house was a block from school and his parents were never home. We spent countless teenage hours watching television and looking at Myspace. Talking endlessly in circles to figure things out, about sex, our parents, ourselves. We had a lot in common; loving but crazy mothers, an eye for art and fashion and the same choice for our last wish if we got cancer and the Make-A-Wish Foundation came*. Despite not always being his preferred company, our one-on-one time was effortless and smooth.

Despite the ease when we were alone, as teenagers, insecurities dominated our brains. I was insecure about

*Both of us wanted to meet Gerard Way from My Chemical Romance.

everything, never feeling like I measured up to anyone's expectations. The only thing I was fearless in was fashion, much to Tomy's delight. He relished in watching me use school as my runway. Tomy was fearless in more ways, but especially in attitude. He had to be. He was gay before it was cool, as well as fat and brown in a mostly white and predominantly very thin school. He didn't have any choice but to be brave. Say what you want about mean girls, but they are entertaining and always resilient. So sometimes, in his attempts to survive high school, it meant hurting me for social currency. I can't blame him; the easiest person to throw under the bus is that bitch standing next to you.

Tomy was always good at hair and said that he was going to be a stylist when he grew up, something he did achieve. When we were sixteen, he told me I had beautiful hair and he wanted to cut mine as practice. The day of, he called me.

"I don't have good scissors."

"I do."

"Well, bring them."

I brought Tomy a pair of cheap black office scissors I found in my mom's drawer.

"These will work," he said, taking out a piece of aluminum foil and cutting it to "sharpen" them.

We spent the day together, just me and him. I felt so special as we ate Schwan's ice cream bars and watched Jeffrrey Star and Lady Gaga music videos. Then he sat me on the cold granite counter and cut off two inches of my hair and styled it. He took his time and made me feel beautiful. I left his house feeling the best I'd ever felt. My mom inspected his work later that night. It was completely jagged. I didn't notice,

I was too focused on how it made me feel, not how it looked.

"You fucked up my hair," I told him the next day.

He held his hands up in the air, "You let me do it, it's your fault."

I should have expected this response.

Tomy would not want me to tell you all these great and wonderful things about him, but he was great and wonderful. He was captivating and magnetic and sucked you in. He was also petty and loved drama, and could - and would - read you to filth. He did this to me a lot, more than was funny and more than was friendly, but I loved my personal bully. When he mocked and teased me, it meant he was giving me attention, and so I would allow it.

We were in the same groups of friends, sort of. In high school I floated between two groups, sometimes hanging out with my friends from the drama club instead (but then sometimes Tomy was also part of that group). But other times I hung out with Tomy's main group which consisted of the kids who A) liked pop punk music and B) would eventually come out as queer. This group also contained most of our school stoners, excluding myself as I did not start smoking weed until I was in my thirties as I was very afraid of going to juvie. Not smoking weed added some tension to our relationship, but he would never pressure me or make fun of me for not doing drugs.

Tomy hung out with two other girls, Barbara and Nikola, whom we were both friends with, although they often excluded me from their trips to the mall or woods to smoke weed. He was also friends with my other high school best friend Wendy. Tomy would ask Wendy for gossip about me and Wendy would always give it to him. Disappointing Tomy when he asked for something was not something people did. None of my secrets were safe from Tomy; he knew everything about me.

When we first entered high school, Tomy and the rest of our friend group looked aesthetically very different from me. They had money for hair and make-up and a less strict mother. They could bleach their hair and tease it and have black around their eyes. With their elevated looks they could prove to me they were obviously cooler and obviously knew more about music because they looked like the musicians. I mostly spent my extra money on food, stopping to get sugary lattes or McDonald's fries, always making sure to feed my friends. My mom wouldn't let me bleach my hair or wear heavy makeup. I made the best with the accessories I had, and my mother always made sure I had clothes I felt fashionable in. But I never looked like I belonged in Tomy's crew. Too normie. Not cool. I looked like a slightly more chic version of the other kids in the drama club, not Tomy's crew. Tomy also made some new friends as we went through high school, drifting in and out of the group. But no matter what groups we floated in and out of, we also floated together.

I called him my best friend and looking back he was, and he wasn't. Or maybe he was so much it roped back around and became not again? We fought, we challenged each other, and we forgave each other. He made me feel less than worthy and not worth his time. But then he gave me a ton of his time and loved me so much even when I was insecure, unpretty, and uncool. I told everyone he was my best friend even though he would never say I was his. When I look back, I realize I am one of the only people who was with him during every major period of his tween and teen life.

Towards the end of high school, Tomy's father died unexpectedly and we spent hours walking in silence, it was my silent presence he wanted in his grief. I was the only one allowed to go with him to get a haircut, he would never have allowed anyone else to see the process. I watched him look at himself in the mirror dissatisfied with the stylist's work, saying nothing but trying with all his might to keep his full Elvis-like lips from forming a prune shape. Time after time, I was the only allowed to see him in moments of vulnerability.

Despite this, Tomy never kept my secrets. Tomy loved drama. If I told him one of my secrets he would tell everyone else and embarrass me at school. I was too sensitive for that, the pain of his betrayal no matter how small hurt me deeply, but I couldn't help myself but to confide in him, only for my words to be broadcast within a few hours.

"Elizabeth says she thinks Megan's a bitch."

"Elizabeth has a crush on Luke."

"Elizabeth leaked her period and is covering it up with her hoodie."

I should have known nothing was sacred. But this pattern happened again and again and for my entire adolescence, I didn't learn my lesson. We would fight and then he would ignore me. I was never sure which was worse.

We both wanted to be cool so badly in high school. He worked harder, so he was often more successful. Tomy knew clothes. Despite living in a larger body, he knew just what to wear to stand out and fit in and had taste that cannot be replicated. He knew about music in the same way. He was the first person I ever knew to prefer Solange over Beyoncé .

One day in the ninth grade I saw tears in Tomy's eyes as he left the cafeteria. He wouldn't tell me what was wrong when I chased him down. Later in French class Barbara, the most popular member of our group, looked up from her phone.

"Tomy is crying because they won't let him participate in the blood drive because he's had gay sex," she informed the entire class. I was livid at Barbara, but I was also livid at Tomy. Why would he tell her and not me? It drove me crazy when he would withhold secrets from me, perhaps that's why I always told him all of mine, in hopes that he would follow suit. This hurt me. I wanted so badly to be his secret keeper. I did not yet realize that even though I wasn't this time, for many of the important things, I was.

In the tenth grade Tomy had a role in a music video called "Scene Boy" and HATED it. In it he plays a model and I am sure that's everything he ever wanted. He looks amazing in it. I used to go out of my way to bring it up in front of people Tomy wanted to impress. It was the one piece of ammo I had to get him riled up. I would casually bring up the music video to anyone who would listen and get back at him for every time I trusted him and still he told my secrets anyway. "Look up 'Scene Boy' on YouTube, everyone." I was never sure why he hated it so much. Being in a music video was one of his dreams.

I have also now appeared in a low budget music video that I hate. I understand. It's cool to act too cool for your fifteen minutes of fame. I wish he was here, so he could endlessly tease me about my music video.

I want to know where Tomy is now. I mean his body. I'm

certain where he is now, his soul is fine. When I moved to Los Angeles, I felt his presence. Although as I write this, I can feel him behind me judging my outfit but also happy to be talked about.

"Tomy came with me," I told my mom once I settled into my Hollywood studio.

"Why?" she asked.

"Well, you know he's very LA," I said.

My mom agreed, but I am not sure if she really understood. Tomy loved fame and glamour and parties. He could hold court like the best of them in West Hollywood. Social climbing, clothes, and partying all came naturally to him. If he were cast on a reality television show, it would have run for ten seasons.

Two years later I was drinking at a downtown gay bar and swore for the briefest of seconds I saw him standing next to me sipping on a tequila soda, but when I looked again there was no one there. A familiar voice filled my head.

"You never take me out anymore."

I often wonder if Tomy was cremated. He probably was because we raised money at his memorial for this purpose. I wonder if he's in an urn and if that urn is at his mom's house. I want so badly to take the urn for one night to my house and have a sleepover with Tomy. I will put eyelashes on his urn. I'll add a sash. I will talk to him about boys and music videos and make-up brands. I will make the urn snacks, fruit, and mac 'n cheese. And then I will lip sync the entire The Donnas album *Spend the Night* to the urn.

I know I cannot ask Tomy's mom for the urn, if there even is one, perhaps they scattered him, I don't know. But

I want to. Tomy would not think this was dumb, he would totally get it. God, he would have loved Lizzo so much when she first came out. Now I want to find the urn and play it early Lizzo. Or if the ashes were spread in a field or a mountain I want to hold a boombox over my head in the field and play him "Truth Hurts."

I started doing stand-up comedy the summer I graduated high school. Tomy came and watched me. A lot of my early jokes were about him. He was proud of me. Because of him, I kept doing it. I knew he would come to the only theatre that would let underage people sign up for their open mic and we could spend time together downtown. I remember feeling serene that after six years of friendship I was starting to seem cool to him. I was doing something cool and adult, but also finally brave.

We spent some of my most magical nights together. We went to my first Pride together, something I desperately needed. When I was with him, I felt like I understood how to be queer, that he would teach me how to do it right. It is hard to be queer without him here, so much of my queerness early on was through him. Perhaps that's why I was so enamored by him. When he gave another girl his attention, I would pout internally unable to articulate what I now know I wanted from him. *Don't see them, see me, hang out with me. I am like you even though I don't know it yet. Please don't ignore me.* My insides screamed this at him even though my mouth never said it. To his credit, I think he heard me.

For my first Pride we covered ourselves in glitter and went to The Escape, Portland's gay underage club. (it is so weird to think I grew up with access to a gay club specifically for an underage crowd when gay bars can barely survive now). We danced all night. Held each other. Held other people. Held each other again. We danced so hard we dripped in sweat, but the sweat was full of glitter. I drove us home at three in the morning. After I got my license I always drove, and I always paid. People at school told me Tomy only hung out with me because I had a job at the movie theatre and therefore money. This was partly true - I spent tons of money from working at the concession stand on him. I now consider it the best money I ever spent. I got to live while he lived.

One of the things I bought were expensive tickets to see our hero Margaret Cho together. I made us shirts using glitter pens that said "I love Margaret Cho" and he agreed to wear one, even though the shirts were stupid and looked awful. We took pictures outside the theatre and laughed so hard we cried.

I was not around when Tomy became a drag queen. But I knew he started working as her when we were in our early twenties. By this point I had created my own world in Portland nightlife as a stand-up comic and found people who would keep my secrets from people I went to high school with. I don't know what his first gig was or why he chose the name Starfire. I saw photos of him as Starfire on Facebook, but I had never seen him perform. I thought about going to a gig but was so busy with my own that I never got around to it.

Since I had graduated high school a year early, we slowly drifted apart. Sometime after he had also graduated, I ran into him in our hometown. It had been well over a year since I had last seen him, it wasn't possible for us to maintain a friendship without close proximity. I do not remember where we were, maybe a Fred Meyer parking lot. He told me he worked at

Perfect Look since he had finished hair school. We laughed at what he had once done to mine.

I wish Tomy was here, so we could laugh, I would brush my fingers on the back of his hand as we talked, and he would stay still so I could do so. I would tell him that as I wrote this piece I discovered he never responded, even once, to the many times I wrote on his Facebook wall. He would laugh. I would then tell him I later discovered he was following me on Instagram but that I never got around to following him back. I would point out that he had seen me perform but I have never seen him. These facts would make me feel powerful. Proof that he was giving me more time and attention than I was giving him. We would then laugh about the scripts being switched and he would tell me he was proud that he raised me into this big powerful diva that now ignores him.

I do not remember how I ended up MC-ing Tomy's funeral (slash memorial drag show). All of our mutual friends looked to me. I realized they looked to me as they had looked to him. This torch was now mine, so it was decided that I would be in charge. Something I did not ask for.

"He would want it to be you."

When he died, I was already part of my own queer family. My two best friends, Anthony and Pepper, were drag queens. They had heard about Tomy's death but did not know him despite being queens working in the same city. I felt strange that we were so close, but so far away. I wondered if it was okay to host someone's funeral when you weren't falling over from grief. I felt sad and I cried, but I also hadn't seen him in what felt like a very long time.

I told my Pepper that this death was hard because I had

already let Tomy go from my life. We were no longer good for each other. I had grown tired of begging for Tomy's attention and instead moved on to friends I didn't have to jump through hoops for.

It turns out, I was the best person to host the show. I wasn't grief stricken enough to crumble, but I knew everyone there. And I knew Tomy. *I really knew him.* I looked around the room at the people who had worked and hung out with him, I wondered if they knew him like I did. There were a lot of people in drag. I wore thigh-high sequin boots. Afterwards I listed them for sale on Poshmark because I couldn't look at them anymore and wanted them out of my house, but I also had them listed at a price so high and unreasonable I thought no one would buy them.

I hosted Tomy's funeral to the best of my ability. I thanked him once again for giving me one of my wildest nights and the most bizarre life experiences, only this time beyond the grave. He was always good for that. I told the audience about him screwing up my hair and for teaching me that cum was white because I had always thought sperm was blue because of medical textbooks, and that one day he gently explained to me guys don't produce squid ink through their dicks. The audience laughed at this, but I didn't tell them any of our real stories. Those are for me and him. I will continue to keep Tomy's secrets.

I do not feel old enough to be writing this piece. I do not feel old enough to be writing a piece of high school nostalgia and to have lost the person in my life that was so important. I do not feel old enough and I also feel that I have lived a dozen lives and that Tomy was present, or at least watching, most of them. I know he is watching this one. Sensory memory is strong, and I can smell him and feel his skin on me as I write this, or maybe I am wrong, and he is here with me now. I do not really care to know the answer. I do not wish to tell you what the palms and backs of his hands feel like because they are only for me. I have shared Tomy with other people too much. I no longer wish to share.

That night, I left the funeral show as quickly as I could. I ran to the theatre where I knew my two best friends were watching a movie. They carried my snacks and rubbed my back. We all sat next to each other, me in the middle, and Pepper linked their pinky fingers with mine in a tight lock. They laughed at the weirdness of the show but asked important questions about the queens who performed. Anthony fixed my eyelashes, which were uneven and peeling off.

At one point both rubbed my arms as we watched the movie and the skin on skin felt nice. I thought about how comforting it is to sit in a dark theatre with my best friends after a challenging day, as they sucked the grief out of me with their palms on my skin. As I looked at the faces of the queers that love me in the dark, their eyes fixed on the movie screen, they did not see me looking back, or if they did they didn't care. Either way it was intimate. I thought about how, without Tomy, I wouldn't have been sitting there with them. I wouldn't have become the woman who sought after and deserved this love.

It's weird when your best friend is dead. To have someone who's every thought you used to be able to predict. Now they are gone, but you still can predict for a while. And then slowly the imaginary conversations you have between you and them start to feel cheap. Like you are weakening the memory by predicting what you can no longer really know.

For me, it's pop music. I used to almost always know what Tomy would love or hate. And at first I was so excited to play him Chappell Roan, who I am sure he would adore just as much as I do. Then I realized for me, she is the first truly interesting pop star in nearly a decade, one who brings something alive in me that has faded since I was a teenage queer. That wouldn't be the same for Tomy. I left my apartment after watching her 2024 VMA performance to go take a walk, because for the first time, I had absolutely no idea what he would have thought. I also couldn't guess what he would say about Sabrina Carpenter, but I was certain he would feel similar to most millennials about Olivia Rodrigo (that she ripped off that one Paramore song but is still cool and we like her other stuff more).

I am sad because I can no longer read his mind on the world, because the world I live in is different from the world he left. He left a world where a Pepsi commercial had Britney, Beyoncé, and Pink all dressed up as gladiators. He wouldn't be as excited as I am for knight Chappell Roan. He didn't go through years of pop stars who weren't brave.

I am certain he would love Chappell, and I feel close to him when I think about how he would see her, but the problem is, I don't really know what exactly he would like about her. I cannot imagine our conversations anymore, too much has changed. This is a new level that my grief has unlocked. This one hurts less, but feels a different kind of scary. Someone I used to know everything about, I now can't get a read on at all when it comes to what we loved most. It's heartbreaking, but overall I'm just glad he didn't have to be here to see Lady Gaga in some of her acting eras.

I now try to find him in the moments where the world hasn't changed. When I throw my hands up at a gay club, I can sometimes feel him doing the same to the left of me. When I take a drag of a cigarette, I can smell him mixed in with the tobacco. I always assume he's secretly listening when I'm on the phone.

WHAT TO WEAR TO MEET YOUR HERO

Now that's a dress to meet John Waters in, I thought, staring at my office computer screen at my property management job, fully slacking off from finishing expense reports. For months I had been looking for something perfect, something that would capture the attention of the most important man in my artistic life, who I would be face-to-face with in a few weeks' time. The dress was velvet, red, and leopard print. It hit right under the knee, pencil skirt, elegant, but was also very tight and kind of trashy. Very Mrs. Robinson but with more liquor and if she fucked someone both hotter and much more interesting. After months of looking for the perfect dress, I was convinced this was it.

I am a John Waters superfan. He is undoubtedly the most influential artist to me as a writer, creative, and messy gal about town. I adore all his films and books but am also a devotee of his artistic persona. I have spent thousands of dollars traveling around the country to see him and still do so several times a year. But despite all my money spent on event tickets, travels, and vacation days taken, I have only ever spoken to John once. It can be hard to get too close to your god.

John Waters has many nicknames including "the people's pervert" and "pope of trash." If there was a pope I followed, it would be John. I will admit at times my devotion to him has become religious-like in ritual. Since John mostly makes appearances now rather than films, there is an entire economic ecosystem of annual events for fans to attend. Many of these fall on or around a holiday, including: his yearly Christmas show tour, Camp John Waters the summer camp for adults, an Easter Egg Hunt at the Madonna Inn in San Luis Obispo, California, and Mosswood Meltdown, the punk rock music festival in Oakland, California that he hosts and usually falls on the fourth of July. I have attended most of these events more than once along with John's book signings and other appearances. At this point I have attended so many that they have started to blend together in my memory, but given John's age and a pandemic, I am always a little afraid each time might be the last time, so I hate to miss one.

In 2018, my first big purchase since I recently got the property management job I was slacking off at, which nearly doubled my salary, was a VIP John Waters Christmas show ticket with an aftershow meet and greet. My nerves were thick with anticipation as I would be face-to-face with, and speaking to, my hero. I had no idea exactly what I would say to him other than I would try to be cool and normal, while I got the moment to soak in just a little of the people's pervert's light.

Now there was only one question: what the fuck was I going to wear?

When I still go to the John Waters Christmas show every December, it usually falls around or on my birthday. Pope John sends me into the next year of my life with just the right amount of wisdom, as if to say, "This is how you age correctly, don't forget it."

As a devotee, I spend a lot of time studying the sacred texts (or in this case, watching his films.) Like many girls with plus-sized bodies or body dysmorphia or who just have to live in a body that's not skinny and white, my favorite Waters movie is *Hairspray*. *Hairspray* follows Tracy, a fat high schooler who loves to dance as she auditions to be on a local daytime teen dance show in 1960's Baltimore. After outdancing the competition, she gets added as the first plus-sized member of the regular cast and then uses her new popularity to advocate for racially integrating the show, so black dancers have the same opportunities as her. Tracy also falls in love with her fellow cast member Link Larkin, a cool popular boy who chooses her over his thin but cruel girlfriend.

When it comes to positive stories about plus-sized women, Tracy Turnblad may be the most important character in all of film. Tracy Turnblad is a fat girl who is simultaneously happy and has a full life. She just wants to dance and kiss hot boys and not starve to death. This is important because even as I write this in the year 2025 ,when it feels like we have beaten the body positivity and body neutrality discourse horse to death, we rarely see happy, secure, fat women in the media. Tracy Turnblad is still the blueprint. Tracy doesn't get thin, she just gets famous and THE hot guy. (I get when movies make the lead find out the hot guy had a shitty personality, so she goes with the other dude with the heart of gold, but let us fuck the hot guy sometimes please.) Then she uses this fame to hang out with cooler, nicer people and to become an activist for civil rights.

Hairspray also addresses the generational tension that often comes with being overweight. In the *Hairspray* movie musical adaptation, there is literally a song and dance number where Tracy gets her sometimes critical but very loving mother to come out of her shell and they get dressed up to go to a diner. I would love to get my critical but very loving mother to stop accidentally insulting me in mixed company, put on some sequins, and go get a slice of (gluten free because my mom has celiac) pie. Tracy helps her mother find a way to move away from a place of shame and into a place of self-acceptance. Tracy does all this in the *Hairspray* musical in ADDITION to kissing Zac Efron and leading a series of events that result in the groundbreaking racial integration of a Maryland-based television show. *Hairspray* has been the one film that made me feel seen and that having dreams bigger than your immediate family's ideas for you can be an act of love not rebellion, if you take them along for the ride. In Tracy and Edna I see my mom and me - as a kid who loves the arts and my mom, who has always been hesitant but supportive. In *Hairspray* Tracy decides to dance and so Edna, however hesitantly, decides to as well.

Surprisingly though, my favorite John Waters movie as a teen was *Cry-baby*. *Cry-baby* is a movie about a nice girl who learns to kiss from a bad boy (who is unfortunately played by Johnny Depp.) Some other things happened, but this was my main takeaway. My second takeaway was that the bad boy has a gang made up of cool, scary, and fabulously dressed ladies. It is totally okay to date a guy in a gang if the gang is mostly women.

John Waters is an unapologetically queer filmmaker and watching his films as a teen and into my early adulthood I saw myself, an often trashy, outspoken, and queer weirdo reflected on screen. In his films the strange and the queer reign supreme, these are our stories and they are loud, bright and messy. In *Pink Flamingos* I loved Cotton (Mary Vivian Pearce) who was desperately in love with both her girlfriend and her boyfriend. In *Polyester* I cried when I saw Divine play Francine Fishpaw, who is rescued from being murdered, not by a man, but her best friend Cuddles (Edith Massey). I loved seeing the gaggle of actors in every film and seeing that a group of queer weirdos really could make something of themselves and that art could be a ticket to a better life, not just a dream. I was convinced that when we finally met, our conversation would flow easily, two queer people speaking the same language.

Pope John also taught me to love my hometown and see the artistic genius around me and within my community rather than wait for someone else to tell me what is worthy. In *Pecker*, the title character gives up an art show at the Whitney Art Museum, choosing to work in Baltimore after becoming disenchanted by the hollowness of stardom and the vapidness of the art world. Coming from Portland, a working class city known for being the strip club capital of the world filled with its own delightful weirdos and subversive artists, *Pecker* encouraged me to find inspiration from around me and embrace my hometown pride even when I left for Hollywood. Most importantly, John Waters taught me the smartest move you can make is to become best friends with your favorite drag queen.

I am 100% certain that if it wasn't for John Waters, I would feel bad about my body, have a bad relationship with my mom, date the wrong kind of bad boys, not have any drag queen friends, and be straight. Instead, I generally feel okay about my job, love the heck out of my sometimes overbearing and salty mother, and my best friend really is my hometown's most popular drag queen. I am still dating the wrong boys but at least I'm not only dating boys. As Edith Massey says as Aunt Ida, in *Female Trouble*, "The world of the heterosexual is a sick and boring life!"[1]

When I first started going to the John Waters Christmas show in 2016, I bought the cheapest ticket. The night of the show I begged the box office manager to upgrade. "Please, I have the upcharge fee now," I pleaded with her through the glass between us. "You had to buy it at the beginning," she said. I cried, not because I had anything particular to say to John that night, but because other people were meeting John Waters, and I was not. There was a baptism happening for others, but it was not my night.

John Waters is a master of artistic persona; he is an incredibly private person, and reveals so much but so little at the same time. Considering he also meets his fans to make a living, he is also a master of boundaries in what we would now call parasocial relationships. I've seen people offer him gifts dozens of times, and he always redirects them to his fan mail address at Atomic Books in Baltimore rather than accepting the items. He doesn't give hugs and he won't read your screenplay. But he always makes everyone who comes to see him feel as if they got their money's worth, be it with a pre-canned response that is sure to get a laugh or asking a thoughtful follow-up question. In witnessing these boundaries while attending John's various events and observing his other fan interactions, I have been able to apply them myself, realizing I don't have to give parts of myself to everyone who asks.

When I had finally secured a meet and greet ticket, I did not think I was going to have a deeply insightful conversation with John when I met him, but I did want him to think I had a cool outfit. Thinking about what John would do, I consulted my favorite drag queen on my look.

"Wear everything," Carla said. "Wear those dumb thigh-high sequin boots you have, and feathers, and a cape, and anything else you own that looks like a drag queen died in. He will love it and obviously spend the most time with you." Even to me, a lover of maximalism, wearing everything seemed like a very dumb plan. I wanted John to think I was normal enough to make light conversation and not with a crazy person he had to indulge. The man means a lot to me, and having a nice outfit for the two minutes of awkward and forced conversation he was going to have with me was the least I could do.

I kept waiting for my perfect red velvet situation to show up in my mailbox, but it would not come. Eventually I looked at the tracking number and realized it was just not going to.

I started looking at Etsy a lot while pretending to work at my job, just to see if there was something I might like other than the Mrs. Robinson dress. Then I compulsively started looking at the same pink ostrich feather 1960 Odette Barsa bedroom coat every hour. The coat in question was baby pink with a metallic embroidery and trimmed in baby pink ostrich feathers. Like some weird addiction, I had to look at that coat every hour on my phone just to make sure no one else was going to buy it even though I wasn't. After about twelve hours of this, I once again made my credit card feel like someone who ate too much on Thanksgiving with annoying relatives: very full and super unhappy. And that's how I ended up meeting John Waters looking like a Vegas showgirl from 1966 on her cigarette break.

I took the new coat for its first spin to the studio where Carla and I recorded our radio show.

"What corpse did you steal that from?" Carla said, looking me up and down.

I knew my outfit was perfect.

The night of the show I arrived early and nervous. I teased my hair, winged my eyeliner, and put on a black and white sequined dress, also from the sixties, under the coat. When I looked in the mirror I saw the extra twenty pounds I had recently packed on. When I switched jobs I went from walking all day to being chained to a desk. I thought of John and realized without him I wouldn't have permission to feel this amazing with all the extra weight. I was the best dressed in the audience - who cared about how much I weighed?

When I went to get into my car I wondered if I could sit down. Would it hurt the coat? What would happen if it rained? If a feather comes out, should I keep it? Could it be reattached in a way that wasn't weird?

I do not remember anything John said in the Christmas show that year because I was too busy trying not to harm my outfit in any way and being nervous that we were actually about to meet.

After the show John took a break while the crowd cleared out. Finally, they set up a table and told everyone with VIP to line up by the side of the stage and they would call us up one by one. The rules were that, for a photo at the end, you could go behind the table where John was sitting, but you absolutely could not touch him.

I brought a scratch and sniff Odorama card from a

showing of *Polyester* for him to sign, which I held with both of my sweaty hands nervously. I ended up in the middle of the meet and greet line with a bunch of other very nervous folks. A gay couple behind me were openly more nervous than I was. Their anxious presence buzzed near me as they babbled nonstop about how they had no idea how to act in front of our shared queer messiah. We eventually started chatting while we waited about movies and what we were planning to say. In front of me was a straight-seeming guy in his mid-twenties who didn't talk to anyone during our hour and a half of waiting.

John spent a short while with each person, signing books and listening to long monologues about how great he was. Each person held him captive while they explained what movie saved them from what terrible time in their lives. From our viewpoint, we could see that nobody made him laugh. It was obvious from his facial expressions that John was over soliloquies about his genius, but listened anyway to be polite. As we watched, the couple and I agreed: long speeches seemed like a waste of time.

"Think of a conversation starter."

"Don't just talk *at* him."

We agreed, checking off rules for how we would act when it was our turn. Why do that to him and waste your money?

Finally, they called the straight kid in front of me. I knew my turn was coming quickly based on how long the other folks were up there. I waited patiently by the stairs up to the stage for them to call my name. And then I waited some more. John seemed to really dig this kid, listening intently and asking follow-up questions I couldn't make out. They were up there forever. What one earth could they possibly be doing? This kid was up there almost double the amount of time as everyone else, seemingly having developed some rapport.

Finally, the straightest-seeming kid in a thirty mile radius and John started to say goodbye. John smiled from his seat behind the plastic folding table as they snapped a photo of them together. At the same time a staff member called me up and I trembled slightly as I walked onto the stage. My cheap glitter platforms clacked loudly through the theatre as I approached.

"Oh coat," John said simply as he looked up getting his first glimpse of me.

I beamed as I approached, exactly the reaction I was hoping for. It felt good to be seen by a gay god. We shared some awkward meet and greet talk, but the few conversation starters I hoped would make us fast friends fell flat. I told him my best friend, a drag queen, helped me pick out a coat for the night, he smiled and nodded. I gave him a punk zine from the eighties on bank scams and other ways to cheat the government so you wouldn't have to work. He swiftly thanked me and gave it to an attendant without looking at it, before signing my Odorama card without comment.

"Well, let's do the picture," he said just as I was starting to feel defeated and terribly unholy.

As I went around to his side of the table I thought about how quick my moment had gone by, feeling the little time I had with him slip through my fingers. But just as the last specks of sand were about to pass through to the other side of the gay hourglass in the sky, my god worked his magic and made time stop.

"Hmm I should stand for this one, so we get that great coat in the picture," he said.

And then John Waters put his arm around me. Following his lead, I put my arm around him, only much looser. Thanks to the coat, I now have a nice photo of me and John Waters with our arms around each other. It is the one photo of me in which I am truly happy with my appearance. I am truly blessed.

I was giddy as I walked back to my car knowing I would treasure the photo forever and thankful to John for breaking his own rule so I could have it.

John Waters's films make me laugh, open my mind, and give me a sense of peace. I know almost all of them by heart and I am grateful to bear witness to his genius. Above all, what John Waters has done for me is grant me permission. Permission to be obsessive. Permission to live in a body that isn't a size zero. Permission to be loudly queer no matter what it looks like. Permission to be wonderfully weird and messy. Permission to call the weird stuff I make with my friends art. Permission to have the love of my life be my drag queen best friend and devote my days to making art with them.

Walking back to my car I ran into the straight kid that was in front of me. My curiosity perked. I couldn't help but stop him and find out what John had been so captivated by that not even my campy vintage coat could outshine.

"What was he talking to you about for so long?" I asked.

"Oh, my shirt," he said. "I'm wearing a Kevin Federline shirt. Apparently, he's a big fan."

Elizabeth Teets

BIG DADDY'S LITTLE LADY

If there is one show that truly raised me, it's *The Golden Girls*. Considering this essay collection is about my relationship to TV, to me these women are like my family.

If you have lived your life completely and utterly incorrectly up to this point and have never seen an episode of *The Golden Girls*, please start with season two, episode six, "Big Daddy's Little Lady." This is the episode that will fix your completely broken life the quickest.

"Big Daddy's Little Lady" is the episode I recommend to (or force upon) any *Golden Girls* virgins that I have the good fortune to deflower. I choose this particular episode because it manages to show each Golden Girl doing her most iconic *Golden Girls* thing. Blanche is southern, slutty, and mad about something. Sophia is quick-witted and mean. Rose is stupid and tells a St. Olaf - her northern Minnesota hometown - fable. Dorothy is sarcastic and smart. This is the episode that highlights each woman as we have come to know and love them. It also has the same plot of any iconic *Golden Girls* episode: the girls, faced with a problem, talk among themselves, discussing, dissecting, dissembling the subject over cheesecake until a conclusion is reached.

The episode starts with Sophia looking at the obituaries to find (very) recently single men to go on dates with. From the first scene, we are off to a good start. Every line is a joke. Every scene brings the characters to life. No time is wasted on filler. When I put on this episode for a *Golden Girls* virgin, it can make even the most cynical hold out a fanatic.

My *Golden Girls* obsession started in middle school and has never ceased for the rest of my adult life. I spent hours watching it into the night so often that my parents joked it would put them instantly to sleep. I've seen every episode multiple times and can talk to you for hours about trivia and the inconsistencies in each character's individual backstories, including numbers and names of children. I love it not in spite of, but because of those inconsistencies. In *Golden Girls* land, details don't matter but jokes reign supreme.

As a teen who had lived through years with a big bad villain of a (although thankfully temporary) stepfather, a contentious relationship with my biological father, and was now struggling with my queerness, I enjoyed a television show where the past was fuzzy. Despite being senior citizens, the girls were all about what was happening in the here and now. Sure, we knew basic facts about them to make the jokes: Dorothey is divorced and had a child out of wedlock with Stan, a loser. Blanche is southern and now slutty and obsessed with appearing youthful after becoming a widow. Sophia is Italian and an immigrant. Rose is from a small town of exceptionally stupid people with legends and stories that go on forever. The other details about each of them are vague and shift from season to season. Like many other sitcoms of this time their pasts, though complicated, were not important, unless they were brought to the table for comedy. For the girls, even yesterday wasn't important.

Despite my love for the fuzzy, certain details were becoming more and more important in my teenage life. Most pressingly, the details of gay or straight. My female friendships were becoming more complicated. I had a revolving door of best friends, growing closer to and becoming increasingly disappointed by each one for various reasons. In high school, my best friend Betty wouldn't hang out with me enough and I became both whiny and enraged. After I graduated, my new work bestie Candace would never make plans with me because she was too busy with her boyfriend, and I spent my shifts at the local movie theatre trying not to outwardly pout about it. Although I did not feel romantic towards any of these women, I didn't think it was normal to feel so severely about friendships. Surely this must mean something about me?

Each of my new besties ended the friendship with me in an abrupt fashion - until Chloe. Chloe and I also became friends at my movie theatre job one year after graduation. Although I didn't consider her a bestie, she had been popular at our high school and I enjoyed hanging out with her in a new setting. Then she sent me a Facebook message at 2 a.m. that just said, "I think you like me." I didn't like her! I had never even considered her as a romantic option. But the accusation left me more confused. Was I acting like I did? And even though I didn't like her specifically, did she sense that I *could* like women? I was irate with my situation and starting to feel hopeless with my string of failed best friendships. Why couldn't anyone be as good a friend as I was and just want to hang out and make jokes? *The Golden Girls* had plenty of time for friendship and the closeness with other women that I craved.

My mother wasn't helping as I navigated my string of platonic letdowns. The more I talked to her about my string of broken friendships, the more confused I became. I wondered if maybe my friends all dropped me because they thought I liked them, and in her attempts to soften my fears I felt like she was dismissing what I was convinced was the problem.

"You pick crappy friends, that's your only problem."

At the time she didn't believe bisexuality was a thing. That was something people "did for attention." A choice, not something you were born with. "But I could see you becoming that because you just have so much love for everyone," she told me in the car on the way home from the mall.

When I was a kid, she never liked the gay episodes of her favorite MTV dating shows, like *Next* or *Date My Mom*. I asked her why it bothered her. "Kids get confused when you show them that."

I wanted to ask her why it matters if a straight person thinks they might be gay. After all, straight people always think they might be straight because society tells us it's the default.

I was a tragically late bloomer - I didn't have my first kiss with a man and finally became sexually active when I was twenty. Despite now knowing I for sure liked men, my female friendships, however, remained just as turbulent, passionate, and unsuccessful.

"I don't care who you love," my mom told me during another one of our talks. "But you always talk about boys. Ever since you were a child, you have always talked about boys."

I never told her about the feelings I had for girls. I barely allowed myself to think about them. Maybe I was one of those kids that got confused from too much gay on TV.

All of the commentary and the opinions confused me

even more. It led to more questions. Did I want to be gay? Was I gay or did I just like gay things? The extra commentary felt like a judgment and it added more to my plate that already felt too full.

Having *The Golden Girls* as my favorite television show was another thing about me that seemed very gay. But if there was one thing the girls were good at, it was ruminating over life's major problems. The basic plot of "Big Daddy's Little Lady" is that Blanche's father, a southern gentleman named "Big Daddy," is getting married. Blanche is at first thrilled about the marriage then horrified when she discovers her father is marrying a much younger woman. She seems mostly concerned that Big Daddy is making a fool of himself. She feels Big Daddy is bringing shame to the family.

As the girls deliberate over cheesecake on Blanche's refusal to bless the union (I told you this is a perfect episode), Rose jumps in with one of her long St. Olaf stories. The love story of Ollie and Molly. Ollie, the town's respected, but perpetually single mayor, falls head over heels in love with Molly, the town's sexiest resident. The point of the story, according to Rose, is that, "nobody knows why two people fall in love and it's really nobody's business."[1]

By the time I graduated college, I started to feel more comfortable with the term bisexual. Nobody knew why I liked women and it was really nobody's business. Unfortunately, it felt like nothing had really happened that could *officially* put me in that camp. I continued to have relationships with men, but could not stop fixating on the possibility that one day I would meet a woman.

I know that deep down my mother did not care who I

loved. But I also felt like she was certainly going to talk to me about it every damn day. Each of our late-night talks over wine seemed to always turn into a discussion of sexuality. She seemingly asked me endless questions, exhausting me. *The difference between bi and queer. What fluid meant. Why I told her lesbian neighbor I was bisexual and not fluid when I had described myself as that before.* She asked again and again even when I was certain she already knew the answer because she had already asked before.

The questions felt suffocating, when I was still searching for my queerness, or exactly what it meant to be queer like me, and the circle of endless questions felt like a wrench in my path. I also didn't feel 100% confident in the answers too, leading to me feeling extra defensive and on guard.

In October of 2017, I took what I called my first queer pilgrimage. I saved up money from my day job at the time working at a Catholic university to go to New York City to see *The Golden Girls* café, along with the city's other historically gay landmarks. My good friend, and fellow *Golden Girls* fanatic, Trevor and I spent hours before my trip looking at photos of the tiny café that was created by Rue McClanahan's gay best friend Michael J. La Rue. The cafe contained an impressive collection of *Golden Girls* memorabilia including the iconic yellow kitchen phone and Rue's gown she wore when she won her Emmy.

By this time, I knew that *Golden Girls* fandom was a popular part of gay culture. Although, to me, it just was another part of gay culture I was obsessed with that was associated with gay men, not gay women. All of my interests at the time - roller skating, broadway musicals, high fashion - seemed to be associated with gay men, not gay women. Rather than make me feel more certain in my queerness, this confused me more. Was I just what they called a "fag hag" in 90s sitcoms? I didn't relate to Grace, I always felt more like Will*.

My mother is undoubtedly a queer ally. There has been no point in my life where my mother has not had a close lesbian friend. As I grew up I learned this wasn't normal for all single mothers of the 90s; I, however, thought having cool and interesting lesbians around was something everyone did.

"Your mom is a hag," my friend Hazel told me once. "We lesbians need them too, your mom totally is one, just not for faggots like you are."

Despite my closest friends consisting primarily of gay men, I realized I didn't meet any queer men until middle school. Queer women I had known all my life. Bi women especially. My mom's friend Jade had been around my entire elementary school experience. My mom's current next door neighbors and frequent dinner party guests are also lesbians. Queer women are as much a part of my mom's life as they are mine.

When I told my mom I was going to New York, she knew exactly why.

"Oh my gosh, you are going to see that *Golden Girls* café," she said, rolling her eyes.

"I have to," I replied, but I wasn't thinking about the café.

I wasn't going to try to figure out if I was gay, I knew that, but I was hoping to find some information on exactly how gay I was. My trip consisted of the highlights of New York's

---

*or Karen, who is the queerest character.

finest LGBTQ culture. I saw Patti LuPone on Broadway and got drunk and talked for hours into the night with a drag queen who would appear on *RuPaul's Drag Race* a year later. I considered, while away from my life and alone, trying to find a lesbian bar, hook up with someone while I was away and nobody knew me, but lost my nerve. Still, away from everything I felt something, truly and undoubtedly queer. However, I knew the feeling would disappear the moment I got on the plane to return home.

I saved *the Golden Girls* café, properly named Rue La Rue, for my second to last day in New York. I took the subway from Brooklyn, where I was staying, all the way to Washington Heights. Rue La Rue was much smaller than the photos I had gushed over on Instagram and, considering it was the only place around to get coffee, packed. No one seemed as excited as I was about the theme. The iconic yellow phone from the show's kitchen sat untouched in its holder on the wall.

When I asked the woman behind the counter how she liked working there surrounded by Rue's things, I was met with an answer I was not prepared for. "Take a good look at any of her stuff, because we are probably going to sell it."

"Why?" I asked, shocked, the café had been open only a few months.

"Because it will sell."

I looked at Rue's Emmy on display and thought about crying. I hated to think such a wonderful place would no longer exist. Why were all the queer spaces slowly dying? Where else would I have to go and sit and ponder my sexuality? Luckily the café served cheesecake, so I tried to work out all my problems with my girls while I still could.

Along with Blanche's father's wedding as the main story, "Big Daddy's Little Lady" contains the most important B plot in all of *The Golden Girls*. And by this I mean this episode brings us "Miami, Miami, You've Got Style."

While Blanche is preoccupied with her father and Sophia trying to date men (whose wives are still warm), Dorothy and Rose enter a competition to write the best song about Miami. The result is "Miami, Miami, You've Got Style." In my humble opinion, knowing the lyrics to said song sets out the true *Golden Girls* fans from people just wearing T-shirts.

After my first gay pilgrimage was disheartening, yet successful (Trevor went to New York a few months later; by that time, Rue La Rue was already gone), I decided to take another to Miami. Perhaps that's where a comfortable and unquestionably gay me would suddenly reveal herself to the world, and this time stay forever. Having seen *The Birdcage* a few too many times, Miami also felt like a great place to take my queerness out for a spin.

I bought my tickets to Miami on a whim while commuting home from my Catholic school job, on my phone while driving (Don't do this - I could have killed someone). I suddenly felt that I had to buy the tickets and I had to buy them right now or gay me was going to come bursting out of me in a way I didn't want. Luckily, I lived through that car ride and telling my mother.

I told my mother I was heading to South Beach for Art Basel Miami, the US stop of the world's largest contemporary art fair. I was still trying to prove to myself that the art history degree I was still paying off was a vital part of my adult life and wasn't a complete waste of time and money. But queer me also knew she had to do one majorly important thing in Miami: pay my respects to Gianni.

In 1997, the Italian fashion designer Gianni Versace was shot by Andrew Cunanan, a serial killer on the front steps of his Miami Beach mansion. The former crime scene is now a luxury restaurant and hotel. As the girls said, *Miami, Miami, you've got style.*

I really wanted to go to the mansion. I loved Gianni Versace; he was one of my queer idols and maybe if I could feel close to him, I could better understand me.

I would turn twenty-seven over the four-day trip. However, I am also an only child, and young women seemingly disappear from Florida more than anywhere else according to cable news so I told my mother I was going to Miami alone for my birthday, two months after I bought my flights, the longest I had ever withheld information from her. Instead of freaking out, her voice got dangerously cheery and she simply said, "Can I go to Miami?"

She wasn't going to tell me I couldn't go at almost thirty, but I also sure as hell wasn't going to go by myself. So she and my (current and favorite) step-dad came along, turning my gay pilgrimage into a family trip. Rather than fight it, I was just happy to be able to stay in a hotel rather than the sketchy hostel I had previously booked. She looked at getting a room at the mansion and called me, "I'm not fucking paying that!"

I laughed at her rudely, already annoyed she was making this trip a family vacation and I wouldn't be kissing any women. My spoiled only child came out: "I never asked you to, you looked on your own, you invited yourself."

Throughout my twenties, whenever I tried to weasel my

way out of the closet, I felt pushed back in. The lesbians I fell for started some drama and scared me off. Or maybe I started the drama to push them away. When we were in our midtwenties I saw Chloe - the girl who had messaged me at 2 a.m. and asked me if I liked her - with her girlfriend at a Halloween party. She was finally out and wanted to dance with me. Holding a grudge for the way she had treated me, I snubbed her and left the party.

On our first night in Miami, my mom and I both got a little drunk at dinner and I got extremely irritated. What exactly she asked me about my romantic life, I don't remember. I couldn't handle anymore of her interrogations and especially not on my birthday trip. I couldn't understand why we needed to keep having these conversations. She knew all my answers.

"I have also been single for almost four years."

"I'm attracted to women and, even though it's not important, it's super important."

"My sexuality is pretty fluid but, yeah, it can mean I'm into girls."

"I have been single for an extended period, and haven't even kissed anyone."

Each answer I gave to her endless questioning made me feel crazy. How many times must we have this conversation? We have been having the same one for over twelve years. I spent the rest of the trip complaining about the food even though I thought it was fine, so I would have something else with her to talk about.

This time her questions didn't feel like questions. They felt like not-so-veiled judgments. I was tired of her mixed signals of what was and was not okay. Especially when I wasn't even sure that I was okay. And I felt like we had talked in circles so many times we had beat the subject into the ground. Her opinions were starting to feel incoherent and my identity was starting to feel the same.

You are not gay but you are totally are but also don't go thinking that you might be.

She was always asking about each queer person in my life. Do they like you because you are accepting? She never seemed to understand that queer people like to hang out with each other, that maybe we had a common identity. I felt like I was back at stage one with her.

In the final act of "Big Daddy's Little Lady," Blanche visits Big Daddy at his hotel. She realizes she wants Big Daddy to be happy and if that means a younger woman, she is just going to have to get over it. She hugs Big Daddy's new bride and welcomes her to the family. After all, it was never about Big Daddy and his young wife; it was about how Blanche needed time to understand the situation.

On our final day in Miami my mom, my stepdad, and I went to the Versace mansion for lunch. The hostess would not let my mother in because she was wearing $200 leather sandals that resembled flip-flops, a dress code violation. My entire outfit was thrifted for less than $20. I laughed. My stepdad was wearing Nikes and they let him in like it was a tuxedo. My mom rushed back to the hotel, changed her shoes, and was back at our table before the drinks came. She didn't make a big deal about it, she laughed it off.

"But the Nikes were okay, right?" she quipped, as we settled into an incredibly pleasant lunch.

As my parents and I sat on the balcony overlooking

Gianni's famous Million Mosaic Pool, I noticed three other women in their twenties. All of them were alone at their tables. Like me, they had come to this place of fashion, art, and mystery to feel alive. I did feel alive, and I was happy my parents were there with me for the experience. When I told my friends my parents were coming with me on my birthday trip to South Beach, they were amazed. "No, how are you going to do drugs and get laid?!" Now that I was there, I was glad I had someone other than the staff to bother with taking dozens and dozens of photos of me in front of the many Instagram worthy Mediterranean-style architectural elements. The truth is, I like my parents very much. Even when they make me want to pull my hair out.

After we ate, my mom grabbed her phone and I posed in front of the mansion's central fountain. She snapped photo after photo like it was my first day of school before stopping for the reason all moms stop taking photos of their kid.

"Okay last one, all these water elements are making me have to pee."

"Me too," I replied.

Of all the bathrooms in the world, the Versace mansion bathroom is probably my best ever pee experience. Five stars on Yelp bathroom edition if that ever becomes a thing. The women's powder room is yellow and as breathtaking as any other part of the mansion. It's also as big as my first apartment. My mom and I spent twenty minutes there taking more photos of me on the hand-carved benches. For once my career woman of a mother wasn't in a hurry to move on to the next thing, savoring our time and posing with me. We took mirror selfies giggling at the images we captured. "Let's go," I finally told her, "we've been here forever."

"This is why we are here though," my mom said. "This is the most important part. Go pose over there, it's so pretty," she said, pushing me back onto a bench.

It is believed by many that *The Golden Girls* is actually an allegory for queer men, that the creators originally wanted it to be a show about four gay men living together. This couldn't happen on television in the 80s so instead, they made it about older women. Regardless, it is certain that there has always been something queer about *The Golden Girls*.

The Golden Girls is also primarily about friendship, and true friendships with real intimacy can be difficult. You have to let someone in your world and sometimes force your way into theirs. The girls ask each other endless questions, they listen to each other's stories even if they're boring, and they choose to keep opening up to each other even when they feel judged, because no matter the squabble, it will all be worked out by the end of the episode.

The closest thing I have ever had to another Golden Girl in my life is my mother. It is with her I have spent hours, (though, unfortunately, not over cheesecake) pouring over the same subjects again and again. Trying to figure each other and our problems out and, in the process, learning more and more about ourselves. It is not lost on me that the central relationship in the show is the deep friendship between a mother and daughter, Dorothy and Sophia. Their relationship is the closest depiction I have seen on television of my relationship with my mother. So honest it's sometimes cruel, but deeply loving and, most importantly, adult. She let me into her world and does her best to stay in mine, even if it is through endless questions.

I searched around for my sexuality for a long time. I found my queerness in many places and one place I found it was taking mirror selfies in the mansion of a murdered fashion designer with my mother. As I snapped photo after photo with her in a place so gay and so campy it is comical, I realized all this time she was treating me like her friend and trying to be my confidant. She was my Rose, Sophia and Blanche, and she and I were working it out around the proverbial kitchen table. Asking questions because she cared about me. She was there for the late-night talks and the deep issues. We would talk it out over and over again until she and I had figured it out, or at least until the end of the episode. Maybe her questions were not filled with judgments, but just girls figuring it out over cheesecake.

BEFORE WE SAID #METOO

In 2019, the last year that I worked as a comedian in Portland, Oregon, an acquaintance of mine came forward and very bravely publicly called out her rapist. The man who had sexually assaulted her, a prominent comedian in our scene, was swiftly removed from all shows and shunned from the local comedy world.

Upon hearing the news my friend Claudia popped into my text messages: "Are you jealous?" I was. Very jealous.

In 2017, just a few years before, the #MeToo movement had changed the status quo. Encouraged by a hashtag, publicly sharing an experience of sexual abuse had become mainstream, confronting the culture at large. For the first time in human history, women could finally speak up and demand to be heard. For weeks after the movement began, I had stared at my social media feeds and took in hundreds of women's stories. It was cathartic, I no longer felt so alone. In just a short amount of time the world seemingly changed completely. Women were speaking up and when they did so it seemed like, for the first time, they were finally believed.

But just a few years later, I was grappling with the envy I felt for those who were living in this new world. I was jealous my acquaintance could so easily come forward and speak about her experience, but devastated that the world hadn't changed enough to not include sexual violence.

"I am also kinda jealous," Claudia replied to my

confession. Claudia and I, at that point, were veterans of this world and its abuses. She and I had both experienced a sexual assault during our time in comedy. Before we said #MeToo.

For my entire twenties, I went out nearly every night to a different bar, theatre, or backyard art space to perform stand-up. Every night I saw roughly the same thirty other amateur comedians work out their jokes, sometimes for small audiences and sometimes just for each other. I loved it. I loved working out bits, I loved showing off my outfits on stage, and I loved how punk rock it felt to yell my ideas every night. What I didn't always love was my fellow comedians, but they were who I regularly socialized with, and there were some, like Claudia, I loved immensely.

I knew I could be honest with Claudia. We had met when she was up visiting Portland from the Bay Area performing on a few shows. We bonded over fashion and movies and most importantly, our shared experience of sexual assault in our respective comedy scenes. Claudia was also older, wiser, and more established as a performer than me. I felt relieved that I wasn't the only one who felt jealous. I was hopeful I wasn't as unempathetic and petty as I felt.

In 2014 I came forward with my own assault in the same comedy scene because I could no longer go on performing in the same room as someone who had hurt me and was pretending everything was fine. But things were different than they were in 2019. I shared with my community that I had been raped by my ex, a more seasoned comedian and almost a decade my senior. After I told my story, I was briefly afraid he might kill me for harming his reputation. Instead, he threatened to sue me, did his best to paint me as a vindictive ex-girlfriend, and then, eventually and thankfully, left me alone. It was the worst year of my life, but less because of him, a man whose violence I had grown accustomed to, and more because of the social stigma of telling my story.

Instead of supporting me or rallying around me, the comedy scene at the time was hostile. Most of my colleagues saw it as regular scene drama rather than something serious. I had not committed any crimes, yet I was facing the harshest sentence: social sanctions. Or maybe I had committed an even bigger crime: being a "bitch" for calling out a man for his own actions.

It is an open secret how many male comedians are known abusers, and some, including Bill Cosby and Louis CK, became central parts of the #MeToo movement's progress. Survivors of both men came forward and recounted their experiences with the once beloved performers and received national media attention. Unfortunately, many of these same women had been vocal about their experiences for years. Both men faced lackluster consequences. Bill Cosby was tried and convicted, and served three years in prison until the ruling was overturned due to violations of his due process rights.[1] Louie CK admitted to the sexual misconduct accusations against him and released a statement proclaiming "these stories are true" agreeing with his victims' accounts[*]. CK than faced various career repercussions including the canceled release of his film *I Love You, Daddy* and broken ties with the various TV networks[†2].

Although neither man faced consequences I think are

[*] Many of CK's.

[†] CK had unfortunately returned to stand-up comedy with far too much support from the industry as a whole.

significant enough, at the time, they felt like a spark that would lead to a massive boom. In my comedy scene we felt the tides shifting. As the national consciousness regarding sexual violence aginst woman rose, it affected not only the powerful Hollywood elite, but small art scenes, including my own.

Unfortunately when I spoke up, the movement had not yet happened and the social backlash at the hands of my own community made me question if bringing it up at all had been a mistake. I would walk into a room I had previously dropped by every week and noticed as my colleagues now whispered to each other or refused to let me join their conversations.

One night a few weeks after I spoke out, my friend Allen, a respected Seattle comedian, came down to Portland to hang out with me at a few shows. As we walked through a popular venue, he grabbed my hand. "You aren't crazy, they won't even look at you, it's absurd," he whispered to me, anger in his voice, "but I need you to know it's because they fucking suck and you'll get through this."

The people I saw every night, those I considered my artistic peers, didn't support me. They saw me as a meddler in their status quo, someone causing drama or trouble. Worst of all, many of them didn't believe me and accused me of making up a story for clout or attention.

"It just seems convenient for her to say that since they broke up," I overheard once as I walked off stage after a forgettable set.

I was booked on even less shows than usual, and I walked into rooms on the receiving end of withering looks I'd only imagined could be reserved for women who broke the standard of propriety in Regency era romance novels. Worse, it was harder to get the room to laugh at my jokes, the entire reason I was on stage anyway. It's hard to have a good set when it feels like a portion of the room is seemingly scowling at you.

Now here I was, almost thirty, and jealous that this woman, someone who was new to the comedy scene, was instantly believed and wouldn't have to face a room of skeptics. I was jealous her abuser was facing consequences. I was jealous she would get to go up on stage that night to a room of people who, at the very least, believed if not supported her.

For myself and many other women pre-the 2017 #MeToo movement, navigating sexual assault was an entirely different monster. For many women comedians who had been assaulted and dared to demand that they not have to constantly be around someone who had abused them, it meant going into a room where there were no allies and no one in your court. You simply had to put that aside, get up on stage anyway, and try to make the audience and a bunch of people who didn't recognize your humanity laugh. I was jealous about that too. My acquaintance would not have to fight so hard to have a good set.

I was under no ill-conceived notion that #MeToo had changed everything. I was glued to updates regarding Kesha's battle with Dr. Luke, agonizing that not even a beloved pop star could have freedom from abuse in her workplace. I watched in disgust as "Praying," the most groundbreaking and honest song pop music had seen in years, lost awards to "Shape of You." Louis CK still performed. Weinstein and Cosby had fierce defenders, and their victims were still being harassed. Brett Kavanaugh was on the Supreme Court. Things weren't that really that different, I knew that.

I tried to suck it up for a long time and not say anything. For a long time my story was a ball of humanity I held inside, not realizing it deserved to come out. Until one day it burst inside me. I couldn't keep the secret any longer and I couldn't continue pretending that there was nothing wrong. I couldn't do stand-up in a scene where someone who did unthinkable things to me was just "a cool guy." I couldn't look at myself in the mirror anymore. I reached a point where the festering decay inside me outweighed any potential social isolation I might be subjected to by letting it out. I needed to say what had happened to me - it literally felt like life or death.

But in these pre #MeToo days, the reasons we assumed women came forward about rape were different. Seemingly from the time of Eve until 2017, we lived in a culture where those who came and said those simple words, "this happened to me," became the villains, not the survivors. The culture saw those brave enough to speak out as women who were bored, lonely or vindictive. Crazy, revenge-seeking, attention seeking succubi out to destroy the lives of honorable men, even if those same men had shown themselves time and time again to be dishonorable.

No one wants to be confronted with a story of sexual violence in their community. It's easier to bury one's head in the sand and pretend that everything is perfect. No one wants to find out the guy they were drinking and laughing with at the bar went home that night and raped his girlfriend. Hearing about rape means that rape actually happens, not only on the news, but to people you know, by people you know. No one wants to be confronted with the idea that they know a rapist, and maybe they even liked him.

I don't think people intentionally try to discredit victims, I believe most people are good. But I do think there are those who have a small part of them that think maybe if they break your spirit, you will go away. Because the truth is ugly. So maybe it's the woman that's the liar, and there isn't actually a rapist in your community. By refusing to believe victims*, it will become untrue and they won't have to live in a world where horrible things happen.

I remember in 2018, when news stories reported that Chris Hardwick was under investigation after allegations of emotional and sexual abuse by his ex-girlfriend, my boss at the time remarking, "Oh no, I love watching his show, I hope she's lying. I don't want to stop watching him." Instead of believing survivors, our culture has long created narratives to silence women and make it impossible for them to seem credible. She's crazy, or wants attention, or is out for revenge. It's easier that way. We don't want to think that the guy who made us laugh, brought us joy, might be bad. We don't want to have to find a new TV show.

Ironically, Louis CK himself laid out an accurate account of what happens to women in comedy who are harmed by more powerful men in his official statement:

I also took advantage of the fact that I was widely admired in my and their community, which disabled them from sharing their story and brought hardship to them when they tried because people who looked up to me didn't want to hear it.[3]

---

* I may often use the word "victim" over "survivor" in this essay because it is my preference when describing what I experienced.

Aware of the culture I was living in, I was determined to navigate this narrative when I came forward with my own story. Of course, and by design, in my attempts to seem credible, I fell even further into the role of a crazy, revenge-seeking woman. It was a battle that couldn't be won. Crazy because I asked to be believed "without any evidence" when speaking about violence. Revenge-seeking because I asked that he be removed from the spaces I wanted to work, so I could perform for audiences, safely and freely. To some, I was destroying his career by trying to save mine.

My acquaintance, luckily, didn't have to face these hardships to the same degree. I was so green with envy, I disgusted myself. I didn't think that things weren't hard for her. It's not that I didn't see she was going through massive trauma. I knew she was suffering just as much as I have and was just as much a survivor, but I still couldn't help but feel resentful that she had it easier, even though I didn't know if that was really true.

My experience, at least in the comedy world, had been so different. In 2014, after months of going back and forth about what to do, I let my friend Elsa tell my story in a group chat that consisted of the core of Portland's women comedians. At the time, I wasn't popular enough in the scene to have been added to the chat, so I asked Elsa to do it for me. Elsa and I had met in college so our friendship went beyond comedy, plus she was respected. She was known to be wise, fair, and gracious with people. I trusted her to be my voice. It was the first baby step in my journey, but I knew there was no going back.

I thought starting by only telling women would be easier.

It wasn't. Instead my friends on the inside gave me updates on a debate about the authenticity of my claim that went on for hours.

Even Alice, a big fish in the scene, who was known for being loud and unapologetically feminist, insisted that my ex was her friend and that she "needed" to talk to him. She needed to ask my ex about what had happened.

The need was for her, not me.

Somehow even some of the women saw my ex as the victim. The victim of a story meant to hurt his social standing and potential. Looking back, it's almost silly. There was a huge age difference between us; we started dating before I even turned twenty-one and he was a grown man. There was also a power dynamic difference. He was, at least by our tiny scene's standards, considered a seasoned comedian with the potential for fame. I was an open mic who was occasionally booked to do twenty minutes at a bar show.

The day I told my story, rather than taking care of myself, rather than taking a day off from the patriarchy after doing something brave, I spent the evening writing a FAQ on my computer. Trying my best to navigate a culture that was designed to silence me.

I do not know what I planned to do with this FAQ. I just knew that I would be asked the same questions so many times, so I should have answers ready. I hoped that I could prove that I wasn't vindictive, or crazy, or worse - trying to ruin his career. People I considered peers and friends asked me why I was trying to hurt their friend by telling my story. They saw him as the wounded party.

At the time, I didn't even realize that I was the victim and deserved to be believed without having to go through hoops. On some level I had absorbed all the messages and thought I had to prove I was a real victim, even though I knew I wasn't a good victim. I was devastated when we broke up. I had loved someone, even though they hurt me. The deck was stacked against me. Still, I was determined to perform this impossible tap dance to the best of my ability.

Talking to Claudia, I remembered the document was still on my computer. As empathetic as I was trying to be in my jealousy, I knew my acquaintance wasn't staying home writing a FAQ that night to prepare herself for invasive and non-empathetic questions. She was getting up on stage to perform a tight ten.

Q: Are you trying to ruin his career?
A: No, he chose that when he chose to assault someone.

After I pulled the band-aid of truth off, a comedy friend of mine with her own story that also went ignored suggested I watch a movie called *Ms .45*.

"Trust me," she said, "I watched it for two weeks straight a few summers ago, it will help."

In *Ms .45* Thana, a mute woman is raped twice in one day. Her muteness is an essential part of the film. She cannot say no during her attacks. The lack of no is not a yes. Afterwards, she cannot tell anyone what has happened to her. She says nothing, unable to communicate her story.

She then spends the remainder of the movie on a mass-murdering spree.

Now, I am not advocating for mass murder, but as I watched the film I felt a wonderful sense of cathartic release. It would have been wonderful to not say anything. To have said nothing and then had to deal with no response. But I still found the justice I deserved.

Violence isn't the answer, of course. But *Ms .45* is a fantasy. And a film that I have also passed forward to other survivors. To me, the movie served as a metaphor. Due to my silence, I *was* killing, but it wasn't a series of men. It was myself.

Q: What are you expecting to gain from this?
A: Relief. Power. But only what has been taken from me. To finally have some quiet for once by getting the truth out of my insides where it makes a lot of noise and takes up a lot of space.

When I wasn't trying to spend my evenings doing comedy, I started looking for more movies about survivors. I needed to see my grief and desperation for relief on screen. After my dozens of rewatches of *Ms .45* I eventually moved on to *Thelma & Louise*. In *Thelma & Louise*, after Lousie shoots and kills Harlan, Thelma's attempted rapist, naïve Thelma asks why they don't just go to the police. Lousie reminds her of society's criticisms of women who dare to speak about their assaults: "and tell them what? They saw you dancing with him all night, they are going to say you asked for it."[4]

Q: Are you going to go to the police?

A: HAHAHAHAHAHAHA.

Not long after Elsa dropped my ball of humanity into the group chat, I saw another comedian I had just briefly dated who had booked my abuser on his show. I told him about what had happened, still young enough to think that just because a man dates you, he is your friend. I assumed he would remove my abuser from the line-up.

"I asked everyone on the show if they felt uncomfortable with him. You were the only one that has any issues being around him."

That wasn't what I was asking. It was so far from what I was asking, but I didn't know how to explain what I was asking for. I was too afraid to ask for my abuser to straight up not be booked any longer in my community of peers. Too tired to explain that not doing one comedy show is not even slightly the correct amount of consequence for turning my body into a walking crime scene. But I was too afraid of looking like I was out to ruin him. So I said nothing.

Q: Why are you saying this now, haven't you and him been broken up for like for over a year?
A: Yes, but power dynamics are complicated, the human brain is complicated and I only just figured it out myself. Sometimes it takes having sex with more than one person to realize that what the first person was doing to you wasn't okay.

Frequently people mention my work ethic when they

compliment me. I usually thank them. When it comes to my career, I have spent years taking pride in putting in more hours than some of my peers. In reality my work ethic is a symptom of trauma. Of carrying this public shame into artistic scenes and therefore my career. Knowing that I will have to work harder.

My ex was a very funny comedian, and I knew by coming forward with my story that I was asking the scene to pick me and what I could be over what he already was. I was not worthy of the trade. Some older comedians made this clear to me in more ways, like not booking me. I also felt ashamed having to ask for basic human decency. Sorry for having to talk about such an ugly subject, sorry for daring to make demands to keep myself safe physically and emotionally. The unspoken solution seemed to be to just quit, it would be easier on everyone.

Q: What do you want me to do?
A: Treat me as someone who had a crime committed against them, be it theft or arson. The only difference is my body is the crime scene, that being said, don't treat my body like a crime scene, I still have to live here.

I saw my ex not long after my truth had spread to the rest of the comedy scene. He was at a basement bar on a date with a woman. A few of my male friends were upstairs smoking on the street, and as I stole a drag from one of them, I expressed my worry for the woman. A few of the guys in the circle mentioned that they knew her personally.

"You should warn your friend," I told them.

Without warning Joey, a comedian I had considered a close friend, screamed at me, his voice filling the street:

"I AM SO TIRED OF HEARING ABOUT YOUR RAPE!"

I stared back at Joey stunned, my body freezing up in panic before I felt overcome with shame. Joey and I had been friendly for years, he had boyish good looks but was a husky dude with a commanding presence. He always greeted me with a hug and friendly smile. To have him yelling at me on a public street was so out of character that I immediately cowered.

Rather than yelling back, I felt embarrassed. Maybe Joey was right, maybe I was causing too much drama by talking about it too much. Maybe shutting up was the better option for everyone, I was a burden on everyone's good time. Feeling sheepish, I gave Joey a ride home to make up for my social indiscretion, even though he lived on the opposite side of town from me.

Joey yelled at me for trying to keep myself and my community safe from sexual abuse and I was the one that felt deep shame. But I knew I had to keep saying it over and over, otherwise I knew that nothing would change. I am sorry he felt tired of hearing about my rape, but I had to keep talking about it or everything would stay exactly as it was. My ex would be allowed to be at the same shows as me, and no one would care. I had to say the words out loud over and over again until I could have a little bit of dignity and a little bit of justice.

When I think of the girl I was that had to keep trying so hard to keep doing what she loved, I feel incredibly sad for her. I also feel oh so proud of myself, because I am certain that if I had to do it all again I would have let it go and walked away. She refused, a version of myself with more gusto, but unhealed. I am proud of her for demanding space for herself. I am proud of her for demanding what justice she felt was right for her situation, I am proud of her for refusing to let anyone take away her stage time.

Q: Why are you saying this?
A: Because it happened. I deserve to be able to tell the truth and feel safe as I pursue the career I want.

Silence is deadly. It ate me from the inside.

It is my personal reading on *Thelma & Lousie* that if we speak no one will believe us. And if we don't speak we will die anyway, so our only option is to "Let's keep going." There were so many nights I had to tell myself to just keep going. Even as I performed for rooms that I felt hated me. Hated me because I told a truth they didn't want to hear. I focused on my jokes, tried to make the audience laugh while many of my peers scowled. I am glad we are creating a world where women and victims are allowed to say something. But I, oh I wish, I would have gotten even a taste of that world.

Q: I need more details to make a decision.
A: I don't owe you shit.

I saw my abuser at a bar again the next week. I saw him a lot. I never grew immune when I saw him. I always felt scared.

Luckily, he left me alone and sometimes even left when he saw me. In reality he could have stayed, he didn't need to do anything. Social decorum was protecting him.

Q: I want to talk to him about this. Can I?
A: So you can get an answer that you like better?

My ex moved to Alaska not long after, taking a moment at a show to finally yell at me in front of dozens of other comedians I saw almost nightly, claiming I "ruined his life" and he "had to move to Alaska."

The entire room saw. They turned away.

A man I had repeatedly stated was violent towards me was screaming at me in a public place and not one person intervened or even asked me if I was all right after.

A surprising number of people I thought were my friends said they "needed" to keep being friends with my ex to "keep an eye on him."

There were so many excuses.

Q: Is this because the break-up was bad, is this to get back at him?
A: Going through this isn't worth any revenge fantasy over an ex.

A few months later at a roast show where I was a panelist, another comedian would make a joke about how I was the scariest person in the scene.

"I know some of you might now realize it, but Elizabeth Teets is the scariest person on this show," he said as part of his act.

He didn't want, "to have to move to Alaska."

Every comedian in the room laughed. The joke was that I was a career destroyer; or worse, a rumor spreader. The joke relied on having some sort of sympathy for my ex - did they not realize he hurt me more than I hurt him?

That night, as I wept in my car, I seriously thought about quitting stand-up. I wasn't sure I could continue, but I kept at it. As much as it hurt, I refused to let him take one more thing from me.

I have spent the bulk of my comedy career with a giant chip on my shoulder. It's warranted. Luckily, due to two little words in a Twitter hashtag, we are creating a world where we can speak and live.

I hope that the next step is justice. But as Louise reminds Thelma as they begin their journey, "you get what you settle for."[5]

I find myself wondering: what would I say now, if I could do it all again? Knowing that my word alone should be enough. That victims shouldn't be questioned tirelessly, especially if all they are asking for is to feel safe participating in an arts community.

I would apologize a lot less.

I wish I would have sent my acquaintance some words of encouragement. Offered sisterhood like *Thelma & Louise* when we were up against the same struggle. I wish I could have been happy for her, thrilled for her that she went through something so awful but was embraced and cared for by her community. I am hopeful that I am a person that could be that way now, to lift my sister up instead of wallowing in my own self pity.

It has now been a decade since the #MeToo movement began. I believe things have changed for the better and its impact is still showing. I don't think things are perfect, but I look around and I feel hope among the darkness. I think there is still a long way to go, and the backlash that #MeToo faced in the last decade is undeniable. As I write this, Brett Kavanaugh is still on the Supreme Court, Bill Cosby walks free, no investigations have currently been brought against any of the names released in the Epstein files, Trump is president. #MeToo was only the beginning of the journey and I think if we abandon the conversation now, we will get what we settle for. I do not want to settle for what feels like conversation, but with no real justice.

At the end of *Ms .45*, Thana's co-worker Laurie, upon discovering she is a killer, stabs her in the back. A wounded Thana whips around and briefly points the gun at Laurie, and instead of shooting her, utters her single word of the film before she collapses:

"Sister!"[6]

If there is one thing I love, it's to show off my outfit. As a dedicated "high-low girl," nothing beats the rush of getting a compliment on a designer skirt mixed with a thrifted or side-of-the-road-free-box satin top. I live for the rush I get when I walk down the stairs of my apartment building in the real Dior skirt I pulled out of the dumpster behind the private university, the one where all the rich kids threw out their belongings before returning to their hometowns. I styled the skirt perfectly with leather boots I scored for seventy-five cents from the garage sale two streets away. Picking out an outfit provides a daily form of self-actualization, my most treasured ritual, my main form of expression.

I show the world my outfits in a variety of ways. Most notably I have worked as a stand-up comedian, so a club or bar show stage can also serve as an excellent runway. I love to hear a gasp from the girl in the front row when she sees what I'm wearing as much as I love to hear her laugh as I deliver a punch line. Streets are also good, a strut through my neighborhood in my plumb vinyl pants can produce enough ogles to satisfy my itch. Of course, since I am a millennial, there is Instagram, if I have finally perfected how to style my floral corset and have nowhere to go that day. A digital heart doesn't feel as good as seeing the face of the truly delighted appreciator of a good outfit, but it will do.

In my mid-twenties after years of romance with fashion,

I felt my relationship with what I wore change drastically. My relationship to dress changed when I found I needed clothing less for expression, but to serve a specific function: to cover up a scene of a crime.

Despite not being my favorite form of runway, Instagram is good for those of us who see fashion as both a function and an obsession, both for showing off and seeing others' looks. I enjoy vintage and my feed loves to show me accounts dedicated to vintage designer clothing. In 2016 I came across the account, @WhatFranWore, a page devoted to Fran Drescher and her various outfits during her six seasons as *The Nanny*.[1] I scrolled through and was happy to find a truly extravagant range of designer pieces. I did not watch *The Nanny* as a child, but when I worked as a comedian I would occasionally be asked if I was inspired by Fran. It would make sense that, as the fashionista of the sitcom universe, Fran would have been the person who sent me on my comedy path. I was aware of the show and Drescher, but until adulthood, had never seen an episode.

Curious about this gap in my extensive sitcom knowledge, I asked my mother why we never watched *The Nanny*, assuming it was because CBS didn't come in well enough on our TV antenna. "Oh we got it, I just hated her voice, it was so nasally and annoying," my mom replied not realizing she had robbed me for six seasons of couture being broadcast directly into my living room.

I immediately grieved for the outfits I missed out on seeing. *Could I have possibly avoided that goth phase?* Now, scrolling through rows of designer statement pieces on my phone, I think about how much earlier I could have embraced daytime sequins.

What Fran Wore became my masterclass in 1990s designer fashion. From the captions, I learned Fran wore many things I love: a speckling of Dolce & Gabbana, some Todd Oldham*, but the bulk of Fran's wardrobe is from my all time favorite designer house - Moschino and its value brand, Moschino Cheap & Chic.

As I dug deeper into Fran's clothes, I also became more interested in watching *The Nanny* and learning more about Fran Drescher. She was so unlike the other women on television I had grown up with, so unapologetically feminine, fashionable, sexy, and still so very, very funny. Who was this comedian that could wear designer and get away with it? Then one evening inside a late night Wikipedia wormhole I learned something that surprised me.

Fran Drescher was raped? Like me? Her too?

Eight years before *The Nanny*, Drescher and her then husband, later turned gay best friend, Peter Marc Jacobson, were victims of a home invasion that included the sexual assault of Drescher and a friend who was also present in the home. The r-word stared back at me from my computer screen, not something I expected when learning about someone who shined with such brightness.

At the time, I had been considering the r-word. I just wasn't ready to say it out loud. Then one day, I started using the word, because it was the only one to accurately describe what had happened to me within a relationship I had a few

---

* Who in one episode appears as her cousin, giving us the canonical reason why a nanny can afford such an impressive designer wardrobe.[2]

years before. I was considering it, only to find it was like a coat I had already been wearing. Despite being accurate, it was still not a word I wanted associated with myself.

As I watched Drescher's character on *The Nanny,* Fran Fine, dazzle across my screen, I studied her puzzledly. She didn't look like someone holding the same thing I was inside her body. It had been a few years after my assault, and still the trauma from my own rape felt strong within me. I had ignored it - so now it was eating me from the inside, and I was afraid it was going to start to smell. I wanted to dazzle, but most days I felt like my secondhand store Marc Jacobs army green coat dress's full-time job was to hide all the decay I felt was slowly seeping out of my pores. I was doing my best to hide it, but I felt like a can of biscuits about to pop open and ooze out for all around to see. Fran, on the other hand, seemed so connected to her couture clad body. She seemed to be not just living, but shining.

As I processed my assault, I never felt suicidal in the "I want to die"sense, but I did want out of my body. I desperately wanted to live somewhere else. I hated my body; it felt suffocating to be inside it, I hated the way I could still feel unwanted traces upon it. I felt ghost hands press upon me and imagined everything the hands touched begin to decompose on the inside, even if the outsides looked fine. I dreamed of a store where I could go, slip out of my skin, and simply pick out a new one. I wanted to buy someplace to live in that didn't feel like it was filled with ash and rot. More than anything, I wanted to crawl my way out of myself. Simply slip out of the carcass carrying around my soul, and into something a little more comfortable. My body felt toxic, it was a bad, bad place and at the time completely uninhabitable. I felt suffocated by the nuclear fallout; unfortunately I was living inside the blast zone and could not flee the scene.

I wished I could have escaped the scene of the crime, but unfortunately, that bad place was me. Because that's what rape is: your body is the scene of the crime. My body felt dead, but *I* still felt so full of life. I no longer felt connected to the meat suit I was wearing, so I spent my days dreaming of ways to escape my fleshy prison.

The only thing that made me feel better were clothes. Certainly layers were one way to avoid seeing the skin I no longer wished to live within? If I had to live with insides that felt like violence and corrosion, could I at least have outsides that were pink and shiny? I watched Fran on my screen and wondered: *Was this bright and shiny nanny also using sequins to cover up decay?*

Draped in an Oscar de la Renta floral nightie purchased from eBay, I sat through several seasons of *The Nanny*. Trump had just been elected for his first term and like most assault survivors, I was looking for an escape. I felt comforted by the short episodes. By the sitcom repetition. The laugh track. The nasally voice. The never-ending jabs between Niles and C.C.

Her body, like mine, was a crime scene. And like me, I felt that on some level she was also trying to make that crime scene livable again. More than livable - stylish.

Like many who had experienced sexual assault, I was living in a zombie-like state going through the motions more than living. While I was at war with trying to live in my own body, my brain felt full of harsh words and large memory gaps. I knew I could not go back to my "before" but I also wasn't sure what an "after" would look like.

The Nanny was a safe spot for me to stay while I tried to reshape my brain and reality. Fran was okay. She was more than okay; she was fabulous. I hoped I could be one day, too.

She had style, she had flair, she was there... for me.

Sitcoms always feel familiar, I put them on when I can't sleep. Fran helped me relax when I hadn't in months. But even as I watched *The Nanny* mindlessly, there was one thought that kept interrupting. Fran, a woman who in real life had been held at gunpoint in her own home, paraded through her sitcom like a goddess. She showed sex appeal. She wasn't afraid to use her sexuality as power. She was confident. Even in the first episode, she crashed a job interview and created a résumé with a tube of lipstick. She wasn't afraid.

In *The Nanny*, Fran is confident in her body both as a comedian and as a fashionista. After all, fashion is a way to say *look at me*. It manages to both bring attention to the body and - if you wear the kind of clothes Fran and I both like - be so flashy it also distracts from it.

Fran owned her sexuality by controlling it. Her wild prints and large accessories screamed *look at me*. But she controlled the gaze. Often we think, women comedians aren't supposed to be pretty, or at the very least, they aren't supposed to call attention to their body or their beauty, because it can distract from the punch lines. Fran did all of these things without missing a comedic beat; I had never seen someone like her before.

What I noticed the most was Fran dressed completely for herself. Fran didn't hide her body, she used it. Fran Fine dressed for herself, not men. She wore tiger-striped suits and dresses made from candy wrappers. She used her body to make herself feel good. To feel pretty. To feel powerful. She wanted to be gorgeous. Despite everything, she was more than okay. She was fine. Ms. Fine. Fine in both senses of the word, fine as in sexy and fine as in not crumbling under pressure. I wanted to be both kinds of fine too.

Fran dressed powerfully. She wore a bathrobe to the breakfast table fearlessly. Her hot pants were short and revealing. Her deliberately risqué looks were an act of rebellion. She reclaimed her body and her sexuality, both belonged to her and her alone. Each miniskirt or sheer top was a reminder of who was in charge.

I watched episode after episode feeling comforted by my new friend. She came into my life at the exact time I needed her, my nasally voiced angel. She didn't only have style, she had flair. I wanted a little piece of what Fran had for myself. She wasn't afraid, I didn't want to be afraid anymore either.

I wanted out of survival mode. I wanted where I housed myself, my body, to go from barely habitable to comfortable. I needed to cover up the ugly cracks in the walls and decomposing floors, so I put a little sparkle on them. So after many, many rewatches of *The Nanny*, in 2019, I bought my first piece of Moschino. I am now an avid Moschino collector and it is probably on some level because it is the label Fran wears most frequently.

As the popularity of *What Fran Wore* grew, pieces of vintage Moschino actually worn by Fran started to go for high prices on resale sites like Poshmark and Etsy. I searched for a Fran style outfit but couldn't find one in my price range. But in my search, I discovered that the men's section of Poshmark wasn't as popular. Sure, it wasn't exactly what Fran had worn, but it sure was something she could have worn today.

I found a 2017 men's Moschino couture suit jacket designed by their then creative director Jeremy Scott. Black with tiny brightly colored metallic flowers sewn in, it had long tails and unique buttons. An incredible piece of art. The men's tailoring hugged my curves perfectly. Bringing attention to my figure, soft and womanly just like Fran's, but in a way I felt in control of the gaze.

When I put it on, I looked at myself in my living room mirror and gasped, "Oh," as my brain began to pop with pleasure. I felt good and sexy for the first time in a long time.

"That is quite a coat," my Craigslist roommate at the time said from the couch, "where are you going to wear that?"

"Wherever," I replied, thinking of my life as a glamour filled sitcom.

Hugged by my own over-the-top Moschino, I felt like my body was mine again. *How could I not want to live in this body?* I thought while admiring my own reflection. *When this body was wearing something this wonderful?*

My body felt habitable, covered in couture and sparkle, and ready to get back to living life to the fullest. My outfit was brave, daring, and maybe even a little bit sexy, all things I wanted to be again. Everything Fran showed me I could be again.

After my first taste, I bought more Moschinos, some Versace, and eventually even some sequin hot pants. I learned how to dazzle with the body I have. I know now I can't control every feeling about the meat suit I inhabit, some days I am still not okay, but I can do my best to dress the part of a fashionable comedy goddess who's in charge of herself and her narrative.

Of course, I am still pairing my designer pieces with my dumpster finds. I will forever be a high-low girl. Fran taught me to take something I already loved and to use it to slowly heal myself.

The first time I put on that sparkly coat, I knew I was going to be okay. Because I had style, I had flair. And I was still there.

MARC JACOBS PERFECTLY IMPERFECT

"The thing about me that is perfectly imperfect is that my tongue is too small."

This line was uttered, without irony, from a highly attractive Scandinavian-looking model while looking straight at the camera. As I watched the video on my phone, I burst out laughing. Of course, this sentence came out of the mouth of a white, straight, conventionally attractive man. Only a male model could see himself as having no flaws besides a slightly too small tongue. I wondered if he even ate pussy.

The video was one of many contest entries for a Marc Jacobs modeling contest. The rules were explained via a single Instagram post with simple instructions. Post a short video of yourself on Instagram, tell us why you are "perfectly imperfect" and you could be the next face of a Marc Jacobs perfume ad. #whatisperfect #macjacobsperfume #marcjacobs[1]

When I decided I was going to enter, I told myself it was for a joke, but in reality, I really wanted to win. I wanted to be a model. The kind of model only Marc Jacobs could love.

I love everything about the cult of personality that is Marc Jacobs, the designer. Marc has *South Park* and *Spongebob* tattoos, a confident smooth voice that only comes with the confidence of being an established artist, a cool and extremely photogenic friendship with Sofia Coppola. In short, I do not believe there is anyone cooler than Marc.

My Marc Jacobs fixation started in high school. I said I was obsessed with fashion, and I loved clothes, but I was more interested in Marc the person than Marc the brand. I watched countless hours of Marc speaking on YouTube, and had his *Vogue Voices* interview memorized. I wanted to be in a room with him, to impress him. He was exactly my kind of artist. I wanted him to see me strut through my high school, I wanted to be his type of girl.

Marc's famous quote, " I always find beauty in things that are odd and imperfect - they are much more interesting"[2] in thick black lettering was the first thing that came up when I searched him on Tumblr. I printed a copy of it out and kept it in my notebook. As a weird teen, I liked Marc because he seemed like someone who would truly understand a girl like me. He liked the strange and the trashy and the unconventional. Which is not only how I felt, but what I aspired to be.

Since I have been a Marc fan, I have watched as he put women like Courtney Love and Missy Elliott in his ads. He even took Courtney and Frances Bean to the Met Gala, showcasing the beauty of grunge royalty along with all the boringly pretty actresses. He had Lady Gaga walk his runway show along with the professional models, even though she isn't tall. I am not a pretty actress or a sample size, but Marc created a world where fashion could still be for me.

As a teenager I went to a high school with a large wealth discrepancy between students, and although I hadn't lived in one since elementary school, I still saw myself as a trailer park kid. I didn't feel like I could ever be like the tall, tanned girls at my school who drove BMWs, so I dreamed of being something better: a Marc Jacobs girl. I was sure Marc could dress me right, do my hair and turn me into one of his weird, strange beauties. His Spring 2006 Ready-to-Wear show started with a high school marching band and ended with glowing silky silhouettes. I watched it repeatedly online and saw it as an omen of what could be my metamorphosis. He could pluck me out of high school, see my weirdness and bring me to life on a glossy piece of scented paper. I could be the ugly and monstrous yet determined siren plucked from the water and end up the beautiful goddess walking down the street. He wouldn't care that I wasn't perfect - Marc didn't want perfect.

When I was fourteen, my mom took me with her to meet a friend for a casual lunch. Being the child of a single parent who had moved to a new city, I knew that the rare friendship date was important. The evening was already off to a bad start after my mom's new friend Traci, a stylish yet tomboyish brunette, had ended up at the wrong location twenty minutes away. My mom was embarrassed both at the mishap, and for not knowing this particular sandwich shop was a chain, and not the quaint late lunch spot she had imagined.

Hoping to make the night and her blossoming friendship a success, my mom did what any woman would do in her situation - divulge way too much information than necessary. Once we were finally seated with our sandwiches, way more expensive than we would usually go out for, my teenage self sat munching, listening sporadically to their conversation. I entertained myself inside my head dreaming about My Chemical Romance or imagining my crush walking through the door and our eyes meeting over cold cuts. My ears perked up when my mom's tone changed. Her tone shifted from conversational to the pitch of someone about to drop their hottest take, a tone I now recognize in comedians about to set up their hardest hitting punch line.

My mother leaned into the table closer to Traci, "Well, have I ever told you Elizabeth is genetically deformed on forty percent of her body?" Traci's eyes widened as my mother continued. "Yeah, she has the Elephant Man's disease."

Deformed? Elephant Man's disease?

All of this was news to me.

I had never heard my mother call me deformed. I had also never in my damn life heard "Elephant Man's disease" in any context other than Michael Jackson buying bones or that movie with Anne Bancroft that made people sad.

Then my mom brought up my birthmark. I was born with an abnormally large birthmark, I would not say it covers a full forty percent of my body currently, but it is possible it did when I was a baby. It covers the left side of my torso starting at about halfway down my rib cage to the middle of my thigh. In my baby pictures, my middle looks painted half and half, like a delicious frosted black and white cookie.

Hearing my mom mention it over lunch, I was puzzled. I knew I had neurofibromatosis, the world's most common genetic disorder. I also knew café au lait spots, like my birthmark, are its most common symptom, but had never heard them described this way.

My mother didn't look at or address me. This was a conversation with a friend, and was not intended to reveal information to me. I don't think she intended to hurt my feelings or say anything that would startle me. She never brought it up again, probably not even aware I remembered the exchange. But the word choice stuck in my brain. *Deformed.*

~

My best friend Anthony was the obvious choice to shoot my Perfectly Imperfect contest entry video. I explained my plan to him quickly via text. We could shoot the entry video after hours at the art house movie theatre we worked at - its art deco interior would be the perfect backdrop.

I was going to enter the contest but not like the models whose entries I'd already seen. After all, I was a comedian and I wasn't a model. I had to, like all of Marc's muses I loved and admired, play to my own strengths. In my case, dry wit and subversion.

Me: *I'm entering a Marc Jacobs modeling contest, and it's serious, but also I'm going to be drunk and have popcorn in my hair so I look absolutely insane. I will destroy the competition.*
Anthony: *Okay, yeah. We'll do it in the good theatre bathroom after the movie I'm hosting.*

My plan was simple: do something so over the top and crazy Marc had to choose me. As I looked at the other contestants' submissions, I grew more confident. Satire was clearly the way to go, everyone posting with the hashtags were actual working models who saw anything that wasn't perfect as a flaw, not a strength. All of them were willow-branch thin and wispy and symmetrical. Most of the entries were from women, but some male models also threw their perfect hats into the ring. Their perfectly imperfect qualities ranged from too small ears to freckles, and then they tried to play off like a single mole near their upper lip or a gap in their front teeth wasn't totally chic. No one dared to say anything was too big. All of the qualities were physical. Each one looked the same. Shiny skin, button noses, large eyelash extensions. Didn't anyone know anything about Marc Jacobs? He was a man who liked women who were terrors. The fallen angels. The wild girls of the world. *This was going to be easy*, I thought. All I had to do was the opposite of what the other contestants were doing by poking at their minor flaws. I imagined myself doing a photoshoot when I won in front of a landfill or a gas station, wearing a custom Marc Jacobs fringe jacket and matching vinyl skirt. I would be the perfectly imperfect girl.

My birthmark seemingly splits me into two parts, a light side and a dark side. As a kid obsessed with Greek mythology[*], I imagined my left side was like Achilles' heel, the only part missing when he was dipped in the River Styx to make him immortal. I imagined the other half of me was mystical, invulnerable, and impervious to whatever life would throw my way. If I was a boy, my father would have gotten to name me; ironically I was supposed to be named Randy Achilles. Luckily I was born a girl and avoided that awful name, but seemingly I was dunked in the river anyway. On the right, my skin is pale and alabaster and on the left, three shades darker, what is called a "café au lait spot." I didn't get the name, but Achilles lives in me regardless.

"All you have to be is so stupid it's funny and he will love it and you will win." Anthony had his phone out, getting the angle of the camera just right, imagining me as his very own Jennifer Coolidge. We decided to shoot the video in the

[*] GAY.

theatre's "good women's bathroom," a vaudeville-style powder room. I was laid out on an antique wood and marble couch with creamsicle painted walls behind me. I laid facedown on the cold forest green marble dressed in a Pepto-Bismol pink blazer with pink feather cuffs. The dyed chicken feathers poked through the sleeves and left marks on my wrists. Anthony put little bits of popcorn in my hair leftover from the theatre's evening rush, and a bottle of vodka at my side as a sneaky but obvious prop and pointed the camera at the back of my head. "Okay, just sit up and say the line, we have to do this quickly. I have to go pick up my husband." I rolled my eyes. I wasn't expecting to have to do this in one take, but I was, after all, a professional.

Now running on limited time, I pushed back any fear, lifted my head, and talked straight into the camera. "What makes me perfectly imperfect is nothing, because look at me: clearly I'm fabulous," I said in my best fake drunk, over-the-top comedy voice. Popcorn was dripping out of my hair. I looked disheveled and crazy.

Anthony turned his phone around and watched the take. For a moment he couldn't stop laughing.

"That was perfect," he said.

If I could make him laugh that hard, I knew there was no need for another take. It was clearly winning entry material.

Anthony sent me the video later and posted it on his Instagram, "Elizabeth Teets is my Queen." The video got a fair amount of positive responses. Despite the compliments, I laid in bed and looked at the video and all I could focus on was my double chin.

I didn't feel perfectly imperfect, I just felt imperfect. But it was funny. Hopefully funny enough to get Marc's attention. I reminded myself that funny is always better than looking any sort of way.

"I think you have a great chance of winning," Anthony texted me.

"I certainly had the best time making my video," I texted back from my bed, eating a single piece of popcorn I had pulled out of my hair. I imagined after modeling for Marc and having the most successful print campaign of all time, he would make me a handbag in the shape of a black and white cookie with a 14-karat gold handle.

~

Fourteen and already insecure, the information from my mother about my imperfection consumed me. I didn't listen to the rest of their conversation and instead focused on the fact that my newly discovered deformity was probably the reason I was so unpopular at school. Since my birthmark covered my stomach, back and thigh, it was not visible to my classmates. Still, I felt even though no one could see the birthmark, clearly they could sense I was "deformed" as my mom just said.

I spent hours in the sun with bits of paper on my left side trying to even out my skin tone by tanning one side to a crisp.

For the rest of my teens, whenever I brought up neurofibromatosis to my mom, she would tell me I was being dramatic. She became frustrated. "You just have a birthmark. A lot of people have a birthmark. The Elephant Man's case of neurofibromatosis was incredibly severe. Stop calling it that." I was a very dramatic teen, and as an adult I can see how my distress over something as simple as a birthmark would be a little over the top. But I never reminded her who it was that called me "deformed" in the first place.

The Achilles myth was no longer enough to bring me relief, my weakness felt so much bigger than a heel. Until I found Marc.

Marc Jacobs is a fashion wizard and I like his clothes but, more than that, I like him. I have spent enough hours watching interviews with Marc to know that we would never be able to meet and have a normal conversation. I know too much and I relate and idolize him immensely. He is the type of artist, the type of adult I aspire to be.

At the start of his career, Marc was a little heavy and nerdy, then he got fit and successful but still possessed all the good qualities of a husky nerdy arts kid. From watching his interviews I learned he, like me, agrees morning TV is decadent, but watches it anyway. He is genuinely touched when people send him flowers. He still smokes cigarettes. I love Marc. He's a romantic without being cheesy. Like when he says he is jealous of people who get to see Paris for the first time. This fact made me happy because I had something Marc wanted. I had never seen Paris.

Marc was the first man I could tell really and actually loved women, who saw women for what they are. Who understood Courtney Love's deep hunger. Missy's beauty. Gaga's intoxicating strangeness. Marc taught me not only about fashion, but instilled in me a deep love of flaws. In his work, he heightened the flaws, built clothing for them. Obviously, if I won he would make me something stunning and stomachless, showing my birthmark in full. Maybe even with an elephant print. Something that winked at imperfection.

I adored seeing Marc's friendship with Sofia Coppola. Marc seemed to gravitate towards women who were saying something real. Every one of his muses had an openness and grittiness in their unique point of view, and weren't afraid to express their opinions or share their strangeness. That's what I found most offensive about the other contest entries - their lack of substance.

Marc allowed me to see myself as a goddess. Deformed? No, *mythical*. Because of him I loved my line down the center, my yin and yang. All that I am: ritual religious weirdo and but deeply secular, lover of men and women, serious culture writer and hard-hitting comedian. Even my body showed my inner duality.

I never thought to show my birthmark for the contest. I didn't think about it as a possibility. My plan was always comedy. Say there is nothing wrong with me, stand out against the models exploiting the tiniest flaws for views and likes. Come as I am. After all, a star didn't see her flaws as flaws, but as strengths.

But I never showed my flaws. I was given the opportunity to do so, to be one of the women I admired who Marc championed, and I didn't take it.

I never saw who won the contest. Every Marc Jacobs ad I saw that year was filled with mermaids not sirens. Perfect teeth, small nose and cheekbones that look good on Instagram.

~

In my twenties, I lived in the Pacific Northwest and my

birthmark faded so much it's there at times barely visible. It went from a splash of black coffee on eggshell to what looks like an uneven tan. Depending on the time of year, friends have seen me change clothing and ask if I had been to the beach a few months ago. But sometimes, especially now that I spend much more time hiking under the southern California sun, I can see it. A heavy contrast between alabaster and buttery dark beige. When I search for the line on my stomach in the mirror, it reminds me of the multitudes I hold.

"Your birthmark is much more visible than it used to be," my mom noticed when I went home for the weekend. I smiled as I hummed a version of a *yes* and murmured something about Los Angeles and my apartment building's rooftop pool. I missed the contrast; I'm glad it's back.

Despite this, I still felt deep insecurity when I had a lover caress my thigh, see the patch of café au lait skin and move his fingers up my chiffon skirt until he realized it didn't end.

"What's this?" he asked, and I paused realizing I no longer knew how to answer. "Birthmark" seemed inadequate, and a medical diagnosis unnecessary and complicated. I shoved my face into his to stop the conversation. He didn't need to know about the spot where I wasn't touched by the river. I smiled to myself as we snogged, trying to see my imperfection in a way that's romantic without being cheesy.

A less than flattering fact about me is that I casually stalked the person who would become my best friend for about six months. Like a killer stalks their next prey, I spent hours researching my victim and figuring out their schedule and routine. I waited outside bars for them, showed up at their place of employment, and befriended their inner circle in hopes to get closer to them. Like a horror movie villain, I gathered all the necessary information, for when I was able to make my move. But like all psychos with a plan, I was unaware I was about to be faced with a Final Girl.

For as long as horror has been a genre, it has been a place where queer people are frequently depicted. Horror movies are where queers come out to play. There is a direct link between queerness and horror; the genre itself can be traced back to early gothic literature from the 1790s and 1800s that brought many LGBTQ-coded ideas into fiction. These early gothic writers expressed their fear and anxiety - and sensuality - through subtext of vampires or eternal damnation. For many queers, a horror film is the first time we see ourselves on-screen, perhaps as a demonically possessed bisexual high school student in *Jennifer's Body* or the transsexual Dr. Frank-N-Furter in *The Rocky Horror Picture Show*. More importantly, it is seemingly most often within the genre of horror that the queers have the power. The queers in horror films get to wield comically large knives, demonic powers, chainsaws, or the ability to levitate. They are most often the villain, but it is for certain that within the world of horror, they are in control.

The Final Girl has always been my favorite trope within the horror and slasher film genre. In one of my favorite horror comedies, *The Final Girls*, the trope is explained to the audience in a distilled form: "Movies like this end when the Final Girl kills the bad guy and the credits roll."[1] I like this trope because it feels romantic, like a version of soulmates. For every monster there is a Final Girl out there who is destined to destroy him.

In the summer of 2014 my friend Bianca had insisted on taking me to a drag ball. It was part of Portland's Time-Based Art Festival, a festival of avant-garde artwork. Bianca and I had both just graduated from Portland State University as art history majors. We signed up as festival volunteers, desperate to prove we "got art." Bianca volunteered more time than I had, so she got two tickets to whatever nightlife event she wanted during the festival. She picked *Critical Mascara, A Post Realness Drag Ball.*

"We can dress up, it will be fun." she insisted.

The night of the show, we got ready at Bianca's house. I considered Bianca my best friend, but at the time I also considered Miracle Whip a fancy condiment. As we headed out for the night I was overwhelmed with bitter jealousy and insecurity because Bianca was dressed cuter than me in a tight satin eighties vintage dress she boasted about having bought secondhand. I wore an emerald green mini prom dress I had bought on clearance at Ross a few hours before.

"I feel like a moldy seafoam cupcake," I pouted. Bianca

just smirked. Everything with her always felt like a competition, and not just the outfits for that night, but I had yet to identify that part of our relationship. My mom described Bianca as a "smug know-it-all." I defended Bianca, she was so much nicer to me than any of my comedy friends. I didn't mind if she liked to be right.

The night of the show I was excited, I desperately needed a distraction. From comedy, from pain, from myself. I was not doing well. I was still processing my abusive relationship and living in an empty shell of a body that had been victimized. My internal monologue was one that constantly terrorized myself and others. Plus, I had never really been to a drag show before.

At an empty lot in Southeast Portland that now hosted a tearaway stage, I gave our tickets to a leather clad door guy with a bleached head and a huge dangly statement earring.

"Are you here for Pepper Pepper?" he asked.

"No, we are here for the drag thingy," I yelled at him through the noise of the crowd.

Bianca shoved me aside immediately, "Pepper Pepper is the host," she snapped back at me.

"Hi, we are here for *Critical Mascara*," she smoothly told the door guy, filled with confidence. I looked down at my ugly dress playing with the fabric, I knew I had embarrassed her. This was common in our relationship: I would say something and she would correct me. Frequently we would fight when she would rush to shame me for pronouncing words wrong. She would laugh and then rush to overcorrect me when I said "antidote" when the word I meant was "anecdote" or "caines festival" when I was talking about the "Cannes Film Festival."

Whatever the mishap, Bianca couldn't just let it slide - she had to pick it apart and show me my mess.

It wasn't quite dark yet but it was getting close. Rhinestone heels and black vegan leather boots filled every available gap of concrete ground, spectators trying their best to look cool as they struggled to get closer to the stage. The event was at maximum capacity and I was thrilled to be swallowed up in such a chic and buzzing crowd.

As we struggled to push our way through the sea of bodies, Bianca and I grabbed each other's hands, high off the anticipation of what such an evening could bring. We made it through the cluster as everyone pushed closer to the stage as the lights went on and the show began. Our hostess for the evening, Pepper Pepper, came out in a black cape and did what she does best: entertain.

It has been years since that night and I have now spent more time with Pepper, who I am privileged enough to call a member of my family, on long walks through the neighborhood talking about our lives and sitting next to me in crowded theatres than I ever did with Bianca. I've had the tremendous privilege to have witnessed several eras of their artistry and I associate them more with friendship than entertainment so I am afraid I cannot give you a description of their appearance from this particular gig other than they were probably blonde and definitely skinny.

As I watched Pepper on stage for the first time, I learned *Critical Mascara* was a competition. This surprised me because I still associated the word "ball" with Cinderella and only then realized, and felt incredibly stupid for it, that a small part of me thought I was going to be seeing dancing, not any type of battle. I do not remember the rules, and (I could call up Pepper and ask, but this is from my memory not theirs) Pepper explained to the audience that before the competition began, there were going to be a few opening acts. She introduced solo performances from past winners and friends to get the crowd riled up for the main event first course before the blood bath began. That's when I saw *her*.

Carla.

There are plenty of clichés about love at first sight and soulmates.[*] I've never bought into any of them. I am a hopeless romantic but generally can walk off most of my feelings before breakfast. Not this time, there would be no breakfast, there would be no days like the one before, because I had found *her*. She didn't walk out on stage, she performed on the first part of a lipsynced monologue,[†] from the step of a ladder, the light illuminating her halo where she sat perched, her face painted white in clown make-up. The first time I laid eyes on her, as I stood in that parking lot in that ugly green dress, I knew that the crazy clown on the ladder was... for me.

For the second part of her act, she got off the ladder and sang "20th Century Boy" live, running back and forth across the stage better than Marc Bolan himself. I stood with my mouth agape as I processed the scene before me. Was I seeing man or woman or clown or 20th Century Boy? I didn't know. I liked that I didn't know. This was better than Cinderella's ball. Whatever I was seeing, it was definitely for me.

It's plain to see you were meant for me, I'm your toy your 20th century boy

---

[*] I am also a firm believer that the best soulmates are platonic.
[†] Bette Davis as Channing in *All About Eve*.

I gently pulled Bianca's arm.

"What? What's happening?" she yelled in my ear.

"I think I love her," I said.

"Oh yeah she's great, this number is really fun,"

That's not what I meant. I meant *I loved her.*

Carla Rossi took hold of my soul that night. She wasn't the most interesting number of the night (Pepper would find me remiss if I did not point out that her performance consisted of her literally walking on top of the audience with dozens of jumbo balloons on her back, literally floating above the crowd.) She probably, if I'm being fair, wasn't the best at anything in a technical sense. But she had something no one else did: an undeniable charisma and stage presence that pulled me in. For the next several years of my life, she would become my obsession.

In the final round for *Critical Mascara*, I watched one queen squat, pull a banana out of their ass, peel it, and eat it. Still, all I could think about was her. Carla. My Final Girl.

I have never been particularly good at best friends. If I declare someone my best friend, I can feel possessive, jealous, and entitled to their time and attention. My expectations for friendship have in the past been too high for the wrong people. Usually they push me away or I blow up, and we break up. Desperate for the platonic intimacy of best friendship I had seen in every movie and television show marketed towards girls since childhood, I had a revolving door of best friends who were never quite *the one*. Sometimes, they were simply bad friends and sometimes I had feelings for them that I could not yet articulate that made me act in ways I'm not proud of. I can be a monster to be friends with, picking the people I love apart.

In my twenties I also fell into the age-old trap of hanging out with people who were not the best for me. Some of that came from doing stand-up comedy, which always has attracted a less than genuine group of people, and some of it came from regular experiences of youth, but overall I was not the best at picking friends who were safe, supportive, and trustworthy. Luckily as I matured, I let each unworthy friend go one by one. They were not the Final Girl, and their time in my story was over.

~

Like all psychos, after seeing her I immediately wanted to call Carla and breathe heavily into the phone. Not to freak them out but simply because I wouldn't know what to say. For those of you who know me and Anthony (the real life human behind Carla), our friendship is now a cute story about how sometimes (and if you are very cool and chill about it) stalking works.

I should note, this was a few years before later seasons of *RuPaul's Drag Race* would go on to make drag queens as absurdly famous as they are now. At the time it was more quirky than it was freaky, and completely free of influence from that television show which I am sure has led to the less than casual stalking of quite a few drag queens.

Unfortunately after my first sighting of the love of my life, I only knew their stage name and had no idea how to get in contact with them or what I would even say. But like any good movie villain, I am relentless when on the hunt. And as I gazed at her from the audience that hot summer night, I was determined to find her. I immediately began my quest, attempting to run into her again as much as possible.

She (Carla, as I had yet to see Anthony out of drag) was living rent-free in my mind as I went about my life. I was more than a little obsessed, I couldn't stop thinking about her. Her image consumed my mundane thoughts as I went on trips to the bank and shopping for socks. Did she bank at my credit union? No, probably not. (I now know her debit card is green and she does not use my bank). Did she shop for socks at the Target near the Portland airport? (She absolutely does and we go there together all the time to get high and peruse overpriced scented candles).

First, it took me quite a while to find her name. In my post falling-in-platonic-love daze, armed with all the modern day sleuthing techniques I had used to uncover the information about male comedians I wanted to fuck, I went to the internet and looked for event photos until I found it.

Carla Rossi. She had a website. I poured over it daily, learning about them in their own words:

I prefer the term "drag clown" over "drag queen" because I'm not trying to emulate women. I'm more interested in Coyote-style trickery similar to the clown's objective - a clown says one thing while doing the opposite. In that same way I use Carla as a tool for critique.[2]

Of course, they're a genius, I thought to myself upon reading their bio.

I also discovered we had something in common: a love

for horror movies. After I found her online, I went to a few shows around the city and saw her briefly; we never talked. I was too afraid to speak to her, I was afraid of how drawn I was to her, how much she made me laugh, and was confused and terrified by my own behavior. Why I felt the need to track her down - it was kinda weird.

I was also still afraid to enter queer spaces and to attend some queer events. I didn't feel queer enough to attend and felt like an imposter taking up space for those *real* queer people. Luckily my desire to see Carla perform outweighed those feelings. My desire to hunt outweighed my fear of not being gay enough.

While I was living in Portland, I went out to do stand-up comedy most nights, except Thursdays. Thursdays I worked my usual volunteer shift at Portland's arthouse the Hollywood Theatre and had since my late teens. The theatre let volunteers see movies for free and all of my noncomedian friends also worked there. For my entire twenties, if I wasn't trying to get on stage to do stand-up, I could be found at the Hollywood Theatre hanging out with other film dorks and eating the free popcorn we survived on between our small paychecks.

One seemingly regular Thursday night six years into my tenure as a regular volunteer, I was sitting at the box office as the audience shuffled out of the main auditorium after a film got out. I was having a good night laughing with my favorite theatre managers Colin and Taylor, so much so that I didn't even check the theatre programming for the night. Until the back of my neck started to tingle. Before I saw her, I heard her laugh. She cackled and the sound filled the entire lobby.

I knew instantly it was her.

"Oh yeah, Carla Rossi," said Colin, "She is going to be here every other month. She has her own horror series now."

~

After that, *Queer Horror*, hosted by Carla Rossi, became a Portland institution. Anthony selected a horror film to show with a queer theme and then wrote, directed, and starred in a theatrical preshow that was always excellent. I started attending all of Carla's shows at *Queer Horror* to get closer to them. As I watched the movies Anthony so carefully curated, I felt the rumblings of an identity I had left behind. For the bulk of my early twenties, I buried my queerness. I didn't have room for that identity, "rape girl" was consuming enough. Queer girl was another story. There didn't seem to be room for both. How could I think about sexuality, when I didn't want to think about sex?

As I watched a new horror film every month, I noticed many of the movies that Anthony chose for *Queer Horror* contained a popular horror trope., The Final Girl. *Halloween, A Nightmare on Elm Street, Scream* - all feature a girl who lives. The girl who gets to tell her story.

According to the "Final Girl" entry I read on Wikipedia while brushing my teeth this morning:

A common plot line in many horror films is one in which several victims are killed one-by-one by a killer amid increasing terror, culminating in a climax in which the last surviving member of the group, usually female, either vanquishes the killer or escapes.[4]

The Final Girl is the special chosen one. She survives while the others perish. The Final Girl trope is one that, as a woman and a survivor of abuse, I enjoy seeing on-screen. Although the trope is a depiction of violence against women, something I think we see too much in the media, it is also a depiction of survival. Final Girls can take anything that is thrown at them (knife, bullet, chainsaw, or giant hook) and they always survive. They always beat the scary monster, every time, and without fail.

I finally got up the nerve as she made the rounds in the crowd one night after her movie.

"I love you, Carla!" I screamed as she walked into the theatre lobby.

"How nice of you to love *a fraud like me*," she yelled back. She paused, "Actually, I'm just a drunk."

A fraud like me. The words, a quick comedic flip she'd probably used hundreds of time to deflect, felt special. I also felt like a fraud.

~

One of the ways I was deeply unkind to myself in my twenties is that I was still doing stand-up comedy nearly every night. Day after day I would wake up, work all day in an office (at a Catholic school until my mid-twenties, property management in my late twenties), and then spend all night fighting in bars for stage time with groups of other aspiring comedians, ranging from many who were casual friends with my abuser to those who had called me an attention-seeking liar on one of the various internet groups for Portland comedians. Some were my friends, whom I still love to hear from and work with today, but most were not. I knew doing stand-up in that scene wasn't healthy or good for my brain, but I just couldn't help myself. I kept returning to the scene of the crime, even if I was the victim. I convinced myself that I wasn't going to let a man take stand-up away from me, which I still think is admirable. Since I lived in a small comedy scene, I didn't know that I needed to carve out my own space, a place where I could feel safe. I also didn't realize that I had been through a very serious trauma, and that I needed people around me who were soft and kind and understanding. I thought that fighting for my life would save me, refusing to let my abuser take anything else away from me, including a five minute set in a dive bar. Instead, I should have given everyone the finger and gone on to seek out spaces where everything wasn't a constant battle.

Sometimes the Final Girl tricks the villain (*Silence of The Lambs*) or is rescued before she can be killed (*Halloween*) or kills the villain herself (my personal preference). Final Girls as characters are usually not popular. They are called prudes because they usually have to be virgins. They are often bossy or shrill or the good girls who complain too much. They are unpopular, which is perhaps why we root for them because we see ourselves in them. It is frequently these unpopular personality traits that allow them to finally survive. It is easier to survive when you aren't worried about being liked and pleasing everyone else.

Final Girls don't know when to stop. They just keep going, just keep surviving. They just keep running, or pick up a weapon they don't know how to use, or try to flag down assistance, even when everyone else rolls over. It is their unlikability and differentness that turns them, and us, into survivors. The faggot/rape victim/shrill girl/insecure loser nobody wants at the party becomes the Final Girl.

~

The following month Luca, *Queer Horror*'s stage tech, noticed my desperation, and threw me a bone when I was working at the theatre box office.

"Should we go backstage and say hi to Carla?" Luca asked softly.

I just nodded at him. I wanted that very badly.

The green room at the Hollywood Theatre is a fashionista or a drag queen's wet dream. A long narrow room with huge mirrors filled with lights. The theatre, a former vaudeville house, has a marvelous backstage. (It is now the same green room I get ready in before my film series, *Isn't She Great.*) Anthony sat at the mirror slowly turning into her. Carla.

I had an offering, a box of Trader Joe's mini ice cream sandwiches. Not all killers use a knife as a weapon. Some come armed with frozen treats.

I gave my offering to Anthony and the rest is history. A best friend was made, and this time, it stuck.

"And then you loved me after that," I say when Anthony and I reminisce over our first official meeting.

"Well, you brought ice cream," Anthony always replies.

Shakespeare said, "Journeys end in lovers' meeting," but they also can end when a girl meets a clown.

I became a *Queer Horror*'s green room staple after that, always bringing Anthony tiny ice cream sandwiches while he sat in front of the mirror and slowly transformed into Carla, and I slowly transformed from a monster back into myself.

~

In *Men, Women, and Chainsaws: Gender in the Modern Horror Film*, Carol J. Clover suggests that in films with the trope of the Final Girl the viewer begins by sharing the perspective of the killer, but experiences a shift in identification to the Final Girl partway through the film.[5] As I watched slasher after slasher, I was starting to identify with the monster, whereas before I was always the sacrificial virgin. In my own life, I often felt like the killer. I was deeply unkind to myself and acting as the villain of my own story, choosing the wrong friends, the wrong environments, and the wrong romantic partners. I was the slasher killing myself slowly from the inside, spending time in relationships where I was abused or undermined or mocked and then would go back for more, creating a string of victims, all of them parts of me. I was also like the killer in so many horror films, always on a relentless hunt. A hunt for love, for friendship, for a validation to end my insecurities with a bloodlust as strong as Michael Myers.

When I think of a horror movie monster as a surrogate main character for someone experiencing sexual trauma, I see many parallels. Survivors of sex crimes, usually no longer feeling at peace in their own bodies and exist in a zombielike state of existence. Much like Jason or Michael Myers we are walking around but not really living. Much like the monsters, we exist living a half life, with two jobs - survival and destruction, usually the latter being a necessity for the former.

My favorite traditional Final Girl is Jamie Lee Curtis in

Halloween. I genuinely love Jamie Lee's portrayal of Laurie Strode as a kind, butch stump on the log. I didn't see *Halloween* until my late twenties and I was fascinated by Myers stalking Laurie and how composed she remained throughout. In class Laurie notices Myers outside as they discuss fate. Laurie feels her destiny. As she is able to see what is likely about to happen she is cautious but composed. I had shared that seemingly inescapable fate, over and over again by the time I watched *Halloween* for the first time. Violence, sexual or otherwise, is statistically most women's experience, so much that it can feel inevitable.

One of the basic premises of Clover's theory is that audience identification is "unstable and fluid across gender lines," particularly in the case of the slasher film. During the Final Girl's confrontation with the killer, Clover argues, she becomes masculinized through "symbolic phallicization" by taking up a weapon, such as a knife or chainsaw, against the killer. The moment the Final Girl picks up the knife is when she becomes dangerous. Before that, she isn't a threat, just another potential victim.[6]

Something I carried with me for the bulk of my twenties were a few words from my first ex. When I was twenty-one, as I was riding in the car with my first boyfriend, a fellow comedian, he turned to me.

"I really question your taste level," he said, unprompted, "you like really dumb television shows and music, like I don't think you have it in you to make great things, you don't even like good things."

"You have such queer taste, I love it," said Anthony one day while we were sitting around and I was telling him about my love of the movie *Return to Oz*.

His words hit me like lightning. *I had queer taste.* Every problem I had, why I felt so different from the rest of the stand-up comedians, from many of my friends and every man I dated. My sense of humor was different as was my music taste and style. Queer taste. That's what it was, it wasn't bad. It was othered. Different. Wasn't queer taste often considered great taste? I had something my first boyfriend never will: a point of view.

So many of my previous relationships were failing because I was expecting them to have the same point of view, not realizing I have an inherently different perspective due to my identity and experience.

With Anthony's flippant comment, a part of the monster in me died. My point of view shifted to that of the Final Girl. The knife changed hands.

I think the most admirable and horrifying thing about a Final Girl is once they pick up that knife, they don't know when to stop. They are as reckless as the monster in that way. The monster seems to die and come back several times in many classic slashers. It is the same with the Final Girl; she just keeps coming through, matching the villain's energy. Both seemingly always come back. I also didn't know when to stop, I kept going out to do stand-up, even when I knew the room would be filled with monsters and that monstrous energy was rubbing off on me.

Until the Final Girl kills the villain, the pain can't end. With his friendship, support and one excellent observation on my taste, he vanquished the real killer: me standing in my own way. For so long, I was insistent upon staying in spaces that were bad for me, with people who were downright cruel to me. I felt too insecure to believe in myself, other than in my refusal to quit, a monstrous and yet survivalistic quality.

With Anthony's friendship and flippant observation, I was able to pause for a moment. Maybe I was waving my knife in the wrong direction? Did I want to spend the rest of my life around people who thought literal rapists were "not that big of a deal?" I had a different taste, a different view of morality, and I needed a different direction.

Anthony showed me to turn the direction of my knife. The perspective switched hands. And here we are, two Final Girls, side by side, and we keep on moving.

I sometimes wonder: does the villain see the Final Girl and feel relief?

I know I did. I stalked my prey, and was confronted with my Final Girl. And into me she plunged the knife of her kindness, her acceptance and unshakable friendship and a neverending pool of love. Purging me of the terror. Drowning out all the lies men have told me and the ones I told myself.

Anthony never says why he took a shine to me so quickly, immediately integrating me into his life like I was always meant to be there. Maybe it was just a fate we couldn't escape but maybe, ever the horror junkie, he could hear my inner distress cry. A Final Girl unable to ignore when she hears someone call out for help.

Slashers, as a genre, launch the careers of women, not men. Slashers are really about women, not men - the slashers themselves are covered by masks or make-up and the women are the stars. It is strange that in order to tell our stories, we have to be hunted and hurt, but still survive. By watching slashers I felt that I could come out of a painful period of my life, post sexual assault, and be reborn in a way. Because slashers allow women to change - in slashers we change from girls to women, from victims to survivors, from hunted to hunters.

I went through a several years long period where I felt that I was existing in a zombielike state. I can't say I've healed, but I feel like I've got some sparkle back and maybe even a little extra. Although sparkle does not cancel out trauma, it does make it easier and more comfortable for me to live.

Anthony and I share a friendship that is largely non-verbal. I know he can sense the subtle shifts in my moods. Sometimes I think he can see the thoughts form in my mind before I do. When our forearms touch as we share the armrest on our movie theatre seats, he takes his arm off at exactly the same time my skin gets too hot from the contact.

Together we have a stream of consciousness with no end or reason or transitional thoughts. He laughs even when I repeat jokes he's heard before. He doesn't correct me when I pronounce words wrong. We don't need each other to be anything other than what we are.

Even when I get it wrong, suggest he do something, done so many times it is cliché at this point, get a reference wrong or worst of all, say something not funny, he treats me with respect.

For our first year of friendship, this was off-putting to me. I was so used to the hyper correction. The one-upmanship from others. I wondered if we were even close friends since he didn't take the time to bicker with me for no reason. I did not realize I deserve a friend who simply enjoyed my company.

People experiencing trauma don't always make good friends and there were many times I was definitely not one. But it also came down to the right person; Anthony is the right person for me. The way I choose and keep friends has also matured and I am happy to say I have many extremely close friends that I connect with as deeply as Anthony (although that doesn't make him any less special and important). I have simply gotten to the point where I can form healthy attachments and know what I am looking for in platonic intimacy.

I also know now to surround myself with people who see me for who I am, celebrate my successes, and who want the best for me and who I, in turn, want the best for. I am attracted to relationships where we are stronger together and cultivate support rather than competition.

I am so happy to have found someone who amplified my voice, and made sure it is heard. I am happy to spend a lifetime making sure I do the same for him.

I don't believe in saviors, and I am skeptical of "I've healed" narratives. But I can say without his presence, I would not be in the great place I am now. So much of healing and overcoming trauma is about who you surround yourself with, it is a community effort and being uplifted by those you love is rarely discussed when talking about sexual assault and abuse. I am so lucky to have tenaciously pushed my way into the right relationships for that healing to take place. To have found a place where I could become someone rather than a carcass walking around, bitter and deeply wounded.

My friendship with Anthony now is a calm one. We live in different cities, but he is still my best friend, even though he has not picked up one FaceTime call from me in the time we have lived a thousand miles apart.[*] But my attachment is secure, so I don't mind. The monster is dead, although occasionally it roars its angry head and tries to get a sequel greenlit, but has so far been unsuccessful in securing funding.

Anthony didn't do anything specific. He just offered me true and genuine friendship. He wanted the best for me. He talked to me kindly and, without judgment, he validated my experiences. That was enough.

The Final Girl killed the monster. The credits rolled.

[*] He did send me a reel of a pigeon talking about 9-11 this morning.

I CAN'T SAY MOSCHINO

There is a tabloid story that has lived permanently in my brain since I first came across it in 2015. Although not inside a literal tabloid like the ones I would have seen in the Albertsons checkout, the still available *E! Online* article could easily have appeared within the glossy pages of *People* or *US Weekly*. It is written in a classic tabloid format showing two celebrities, Kesha and Rihanna, wearing the same dress. The garment in question: a slim-fitting ankle length dress with the words "You Will Never Own Me" spelled out in bright sequins.

"Bitch Stole My Look" reads the first part of the headline under the photos of the two singers. I knew this particular line was one of Joan Rivers's slogans from her show *Fashion Police*, which aired on the E! Network at the time, but nevertheless I found the headline exceptionally dense. The article failed to mention the obvious context behind the outfit: both of these women were survivors of abuse with public discourse surrounding their experiences. Kesha was still in the middle of her series of lawsuits with her former producer Dr. Luke, whom she had alleged had emotionally abused as well as drugged and raped her on two different occasions. Rihanna had been the focus of tabloid gossip for her relationship with Chris Brown that included a 2009 domestic abuse incident that left her with visible facial injuries that required medical attention.

The subtitle reads, "Yikes! Check out this pop star

fashion face off" and contains a poll to vote which pop star wore the dress better.[1] I laughed at the irony, who knows how long the same tabloid industry had been covering, and therefore profiting off, these women's traumas. But when it came to what was obviously a fashion statement in opposition of both the abuse they faced and the surrounding attention, the article seemed to forget all about these women's histories and instead wanted, like it often does, to create competition between women - this time for wearing the same outfit.[*]

For years, I had seen dozens of cover stories about Rihanna's domestic abuse and massive media coverage of Kesha's court case against Dr. Luke. Despite the seemingly infinite amount of coverage, the article missed the parallel between these women's stories and the context for this piece of fashion. This dress, by the brand Discount Universe wasn't just another dazzling piece; it was an intentional declaration - perhaps even to the media that was profiting off of their stories itself.

Before I stumbled across the tabloid article, I was familiar with the dress in question. I had made that same photo of Kesha my Facebook cover photo. For those unfamiliar with the social media culture of 2015, a Facebook cover photo appeared on one's profile page above one's profile picture. Most people uploaded something scenic or to express their personality in this photo slot. My choice to publicly display this particular photo of Kesha wearing the dress was intentional as an extension of my online footprint. She faces the camera with a confident expression, the dress's front slogan on full

---

[*] The back of the dress also included the words "I Will Never Fear You."

display. At the time I was active in my city's comedy scene, and having just outed a fellow comedian for sexually assaulting me, I felt a kinship with the pop star, as I was now having to face my own version of the court of public opinion.

In 2018, I took out my credit card and purchased the Discount Universe* dress for myself. I wanted to feel like what had happened to me "would never own me," that I was not defined by my trauma. I wanted to feel in control despite facing the court of public opinion just as Kesha and Rihanna. I could not afford that dress. I make almost twice what I did in 2018 and I still cannot afford that dress. Despite my bank account's protests, I felt like I couldn't afford not to have it, so much that I bought it at full price, something I almost never do.

What I wore had become a way to feel safe and take back control of my experience living in my own body. I cannot control what happened to my fleshy prison, but I can control what's on it. I thought that perhaps buying the "You Will Never Own Me" dress would change something in me. That it would heal me from the outside in. My instincts were incorrect in this case, but they weren't far off. I was right about one thing: my wardrobe needed statement pieces. I wanted my clothing to say something, to speak to me and to the world. That dress was a stop on my journey leading me to what I really needed when it comes to fashion.

When I get dressed, I want what I put on my body to mean something, and what I want on my body more than

---

*The version available online for purchase was slightly different from the original in shape and color and did not have words on the back.

anything, more than expensive night creams, or diamonds, or handsome men with biceps, is Moschino.

Because Moschino knows how to make a statement.

When the Italian designer Franco Moschino launched his label in 1986, his first collection made a splash for its intentional mockery of the fashion industry. He brought cheekiness and wit to the runway by redesigning classics from powerhouse fashion houses - like the Chanel suit - and adding his own humor. In Moschino's world, skirts are made out of executives' neckties, dresses resemble the brushes inside your neighborhood car wash, and sometimes the hard plastic of dozens of shopping tags stuck inside the top aren't a mistake - they are meant to be left on for decoration. Franco found the backs of those classic suit jackets are the perfect place for a smattering of wit or a three word manifesto. Each piece of Moschino feels like a smug smile directed at the upper classes who feel defined by classic cuts with a designer label.

In a 1990 *Vanity Fair* interview Moschino mused that he was "more like a political cartoonist, sending up established symbols of power and affluence."[2] I recently came across a Reddit thread where one lucky Moschino thrifter discovered a secret comic strip sewn into a seemingly basic, black blazer. It is this whimsy and trickery that attracted me to Franco's work. Franco taught me fashion can be a prank, fashion can be trouble, fashion can be unruly, and that the best way to handle chaos or injustice, is to face it head on…and grin. Facing everything grim and surreal in this world with a smile and a wink feels like the best way to manage.

My body felt unruly. The world felt like mayhem wrapped in plastic. So why shouldn't my clothes reflect that through glamour? Living in a world where one in three women experience sexual violence is absurd; I wanted my clothes that house my tender body to reflect some form of absurdity. Why shouldn't my dress look like a car wash brush? Shouldn't I be allowed to look absurd when I live on an insane planet? Matching the ludicrousness with clothing felt invigorating. The point of a political cartoon is to make commentary on events, and my body felt like the perfect place for the conversation. After all, what's more political than a woman's body? What's more political than the way a woman spends her money?

When I look at Franco's work, I feel my teenage rebellion come out, but in a way that is mixed in with the attitude of the adult woman I was forced to become. My rebellion has to be smart, and cut through noise with a smirk, rather than a scream. There is a power in that smirk, only those who get the joke know why you are wearing it, both the smirk and T-shirt dress that reads "For Fashion Victims Only" across the front.

Jeremy Scott, Moschino's creative director from 2013 to 2023, expanded on Franco's legacy with an explosive pop. He took many of Franco's original ideas and added exaggerated pop culture references. Classically tailored suits inspired by McDonald's uniforms, silhouettes meant to resemble candy bar wrappers, and runway dresses meant to make the wearer look like a TV dinner. As a girl who always let her pop culture obsessions lead the way, Jeremy Scott felt like my fashion soulmate in every way a designer could.

I think the reason the "You Will Never Own Me" dress didn't feel the same, was that it felt too loud, too direct. When it comes to changing - be it the minds of others or my own mind - I have always preferred humor as my weapon of choice. The "You Will Never Own Me" dress felt forced. As much as I am all for a statement spelled out in sequins, I need the message to be served with a hint of mischief - a bit of sardonic wit goes further than a scream. I don't want to spend the rest of my life yelling, but I don't want to be silent either.

Moschino aims to make trouble, and so do I. Where Franco brought subversion and irony, Jeremy Scott brought joy. My favorite dress is a simple white mini dress that is meant to look like it was scribbled on with a giant pink highlighter. When I wear it I sometimes imagine a giant toddler gripping a jumbo neon Bic, scribbling on me like I'm Polly Pocket. Through them I found other ways to deliver my message with my fashion choices, the Moschino way, with wry humor and a bit of fun.

Franco's subversive humor taught me that fashion wasn't only commerce and fabric, but could be a form of parody and satire. Fashion can be more than beauty. His pieces mock their buyer, often literally and his shapes make puns. Many of his pieces feature the word "cheap*" in big block letters, as if daring the affluent upper class buyer to walk down the street with the offensive word on their back. My longest search for a piece designed by Franco was a fringe dress with the words "Read Between The Lines" printed on the tassels. It never fails to make me chuckle under my breath. The dress hangs in my closet, a reminder it's okay to look like a joke as long as you're the one making it.

Jeremy Scott, in equal measure, has brought a subtler but more whimsical humor into my life and wardrobe. His designs

*Especially for the Moschino Cheap and Chic label.

I am most drawn to are equal parts camp and glamour. I own two dresses from his 2015 show inspired by Barbie. I've never asked myself if I am too old or the wrong shape to wear them; there I feel like the "bimbo friend" I always wanted to be as a kid listening to Aqua in my mom's Toyota. Most of Scott's pieces do not mock the affluent buyer as openly - Scott, like me, is from a suburban background and when I wear his pieces, I feel a type of kinship with him. Together we are two American artists who somehow cheated the system and got ourselves into couture clothing.

For a long time, a new outfit was the only thing keeping me alive and sane in my body. It was my own form of therapy, but, much like deadheading a plant, healing can also be a form of self-destruction. For the bulk of my late twenties, I became an obsessive Moschino collector. I spent endless hours on resale sites and in vintage stores digging for the next ironic fringe sleeve coat or campy plastic top to add to my wardrobe. I felt a rush each time I came across a rare gem for my collection, and then the need to do it again.

Each time, I felt a little healed and a little more sure of myself. Then with each swipe of my card, I added to my debt and dug myself a little deeper into the hole. Many other Moschino collectors I have met are not people who can afford couture clothing. I can only say for myself, but I think we continue to collect rare pieces at sometimes extravagant prices because we feel in on the joke. After all, Franco's 1991 collection featured an apple red Chanel style suit embroidered with the words "Waist of Money." Moschino has always been unafraid to address class directly.

I became a Moschino junkie from watching *The Nanny*, but

at the time *The Nanny* was airing, my young heart had already found one gravelly-voiced fashion goddess, Julie Kavner, who enraptured me both as my idol Dottie Ingels in *This Is My Life* and as the voice of Marge Simpson. As a *Simpsons* junkie I watched reruns every night after school hoping to see a repeat of my favorite episode. In "Scenes from the Class Struggle in Springfield," the fourteenth episode in the seventh season of *The Simpsons*, Marge makes a spectacular find at a bargain store: a pink Chanel suit.

The first time I saw Marge in that suit, I was changed forever. Even though it was animated, you could see the lines were cut to the body to look flattering. Even on a cartoon yellow one. As a kindergartener watching Marge admire herself in the mirror, my future as a high-low fashion girl was formed.

Through Marge's Chanel suit, I learned there were special clothes, different from all other clothes. These clothes could get you things and convince people you deserved to be treated a certain way. These clothes could convey a message without words. And most importantly, you could get them on sale if you were willing to look for them.

Through her new suit, Marge is able to social climb and begins to receive attention from the higher classes of Springfield, getting invited to the country club and other outings. Since she only has the one designer outfit, each night Marge spends hours at her sewing machine reconstructing the Chanel suit into new creations.[3] Like Franco, *The Simpsons* also deconstructs a classic Chanel silhouette for comedy. It is perhaps Marge's fault that I am more attracted to a mocking redesign than I am to a classic piece of couture.

Of course, the message of "Scenes from the Class Struggle in Springfield" is that the Chanel suit gets Marge and her family in with Springfield's elite - people who wouldn't have noticed them had Marge not found the suit marked down to $90 from $2800. This is supposed to be a cautionary tale, but all I learned was to stay away from country clubs.

Despite getting the suit for a discount, Marge changes as a person; she ends up buying another designer piece (after accidentally destroying her suit when it gets caught in her sewing machine). Although Marge realizes her mistake, it is only after she ends up buying a second dress and ends up with a huge credit at Chanel. Like Marge, I fell down the designer rabbit hole at a bargain price but ended up paying in full in the long run.

I often wonder what Franco Moschino would think of some girl getting into actual debt to buy his clothing. I assume a part of him would be sad, that I missed his humor, that I wasn't in on the joke. Maybe the irony is I was so in on it that I didn't realize the joke was now on me. I know Franco loved irony. In 1991 he showed a simple white shirt with the words "Too Much Irony!" on the back, visible when the wearer turns around, along with a literal stain from an actual iron. I love irony, but the irony is that I'm dressing my traumatized body in clothes that I can't afford, creating a loop of destruction.

There is a tutu dress Jeremy Scott showed during his time at the brand with the text "It's Very Expensive Being Moschino," a piece that feels so tailored to me, I cannot debase myself enough to buy it, even though its self-deprecating directedness would entertain me for at least the rest of the decade.

Franco Moschino both adored and made fun of luxury fashion once stating, "Funny clothes have to be extremely well made because that is where you find the chic. It's easy to be funny with a T-shirt, but it's more clever with a mink coat. After all, if caviar was cheaper, it would taste much less interesting."[4]

I am grateful for both of my Moschino daddies. Their art has given me a reason to want to leave the house when I feel like a walking crime scene and make me feel special and worthy. Because when I'm wearing Moschino, I feel like the most interesting girl in the world.

Franco taught me about subversion, a tool to question power, when I needed something to feel like the world we live in, that so easily let women's bodies be harmed without a blink of an eye, needed to be questioned. Jeremy Scott brought fun and silliness into my world and my closet. This silliness and campy sensibility has healed me from the outside in. It is truly hard to be sad when you are dressing up. They taught me clothes don't have to be serious to be evocative and innovative. They taught me that I don't have to be serious to be evocative or interesting. It is hard to look at one's body in the mirror and see something broken or ugly or undesirable, when you are wearing a dress designed to make the wearer appear as if they are a giant bouquet of flowers.

My Moschino collection has grown piece by piece. My hangers are filled with pop art print jackets, telephone book trousers, embellished tailcoats, scribbled-on mini skirts, and trompe l'oeil blazers. When I look in my closet, I feel warm and melty and like a bubble about to pop all at the same time.

My collection is my ultimate fantasy. I created the

wardrobe of my dreams and I worked hard to make it happen. I like how it makes me feel to be the person who collects and owns each piece and knows their history. It gives me a sense of pride and purpose. I am smart, sophisticated, sexy and subversive. I am a girl cool and smart enough to love these clothes.

Moschino will always be my main addiction. I hate being drunk, three martinis don't do it for me; I prefer to wear big coats to decompress and the effect on my bloodstream is the same. The fabric drapes around me and my blood starts to pop with fizzling pleasure. The pieces of my Moschino car wash dress move with me as I shimmy. I like being looked at for artistic choices I made rather than feeling like I'm being leered at because I have triple Ds. I like having my photo taken in couture that I purchased with *my* money. I like to remember that dinner I went to where I wore that great outfit. I like feeling good in my body and in the world. I like not thinking about how this body was raped.

Got trauma? Cover it with couture!

When I fall in love with a piece of vintage Moschino, I have a hard time saying no. Especially if it's priced well below retail, I convince myself, as Marge said with the marked down Chanel, "It'll be good for the economy."[5] I like looking like I can afford something expensive. I like tricking people about what social class I'm in. I like performing the role of a well-dressed writer. And most importantly, I like it when the fabric touches me, it's safe and feels good on my skin. Every single part of the experience is intoxicating. I cannot imagine anything better.

Jeremy Scott and Franco Moschino created a world of

fashion so perfect that I allowed myself to drown in it. In dresses that make the wearer look like a six layer cake or a dry cleaner bag or a slot machine. They allowed me back in my body as a girl playing dress-up, a girl who could be anything even when it felt like everything was taken from her.

More intoxicating than getting a fabulous piece of couture is the hunt for it. I have never purchased a piece of designer clothing at full price. Everything comes through intense hunting and looking and collecting of deals and discount codes and bargaining back and forth with Depop or Ebay sellers.

I also feel a sense of working class morality over getting a bargain on a designer piece. I have multiple pieces of Moschino that are also featured in the permanent collection at the Metropolitan Museum of Art. Somehow by owning these pieces of clothing, I have managed to pull one over on the upper classes. But if you do this enough, which I have, the debts can still rack up - a $2,000 jacket purchased at only $200 twenty times, because I can't stop doing it, is still $20,000. Now I have a pile of debt and an impressive collection of rare pieces whose estimated value I don't even know.

I do not recommend getting into massive amounts of debt if you aren't doing so for a reason, although I think there are many good reasons to do so. Healing from my body trauma is my reason, and for that, I am not sorry that I bought as many clothes as I have over the years. But this way of living is no longer healing me; it is now hurting. As much as I enjoy my collection, and for a while it was the only thing keeping me alive, it became a form of self-destruction.

There is a rather famous Moschino dress - the silhouette

of a red traffic sign with the words changed from "Stop" to "Shop." It's funny and also a joke that hits a little too close to home.

But knowing me, I will probably add it to my collection at some point. I like to be in on the joke.

Elizabeth Teets

CARRIE'S CREDIT CARDS

I am certain there is a significant number of women who have had their credit scores ruined by the money habits of Carrie Bradshaw. There are a lot of us out there inspired by our favorite on-screen single girl fashionista with a lot of designer clothes, and therefore a lot of credit card debt.

Carrie Bradshaw, the protagonist of *Sex and the City*, is in many ways the blueprint for every city girl who still finds themselves single past the age of thirty and still seeking love, sex, and a fulfilling career. She is also a fictional character who still evokes strong opinions in the cultural zeitgeist despite having first appeared more than twenty-five years ago, and whose actions have been analyzed and written about to death on the internet - be it on her relationship styles, curly hair, the show's complete lack of diversity, or the debate of whether or not she is a good person - as if that even matters. But Carrie's impact on both modern women, and especially women writers, cannot be understated.

Whereas Fran Fine gave me a taste for fashion as fun, Carrie gave me a taste for designer as a form of power. Carrie wore labels and through her, I learned labels had meaning. Clothes became not only things to wear but art and a signifier of taste, elegance, and, of course, social class. All of this came with a price tag.

Despite her love for labels, Carrie, like myself, is a high-low girl. A woman who mixes pieces from a few favorite designers (for Carrie, Manolo Blahnik and Jimmy Choo; for me, Moschino and Marc Jacobs), with pieces from thrift shops and vintage finds. As Carrie once perfectly put it: "I was looking for a perfect seven dollar vintage dress to go with my four hundred dollar shoes."[1]

I am a writer, single girl, and fashion lover. I love Carrie Bradshaw and I will not apologize. As a writer in a major city who spends many of her nights out on the town and her days off lying in bed with a copy of *Vogue* and often a matching Parisian Vogue cigarette - her impact on lifestyle, wardrobe and career is undeniable. She showed me what it means to be a big city girl. She has also granted me permission to behave badly more than any other real or fictional character, and some of that bad behavior is in the form of poor money habits.

In *Sex and The City* season four, episode sixteen, "Ring a Ding Ding," after breaking up with the lesser great love of her life Aidan, Carrie is faced with the conundrum of having to buy her fabulous apartment back from her ex-boyfriend on short notice after a break-up. As she attempts to come up with a down payment and examines her money habits, she discovers that she has around one hundred pairs of Manolo Blahniks, and at around four hundred bucks a pair, she has $40,000 in shoes - and no place to live.[2] That's the thing about designer fashion and credit cards: one big purchase feels great.

I'll pay it off over time, I think every time I enter my Amex number or tap and hold at the vintage shop. Then I do it again and again and suddenly an almost ten thousand dollar tab stares back at me. I open my closet and see a small fortune, but I also think to myself: look at who I have become, the fabulous woman to whom this wardrobe belongs. The chic and sophisticated woman I dreamed of becoming one day. When I look at what marvels cling to the hangers inside my closet the bill doesn't feel so bad.

I love *Sex and the City*. I bow down to its influence on me and seemingly every other woman I've ever met who chose a big city over a suburban one. Its impact on my life is unmatched. I don't feel bad that I don't have a partner and children because I have a full closet, a full social calendar, and a full life. I am now a thirty-something-year-old single woman living in a major city who has spent many nights in front of my laptop writing and wondering. Although as an optimist and art history major, I identify more as a Charlotte, but there is always a soft spot in my heart for my fashionista writer matriarch for teaching me what is possible in this life: a few bylines in my favorite magazines, a couple rich ex-boyfriends, a closet full of clothes, and a credit report full of debt to pay for them.

I already know my mother is going to read this essay, put this book down, and call me to demand to know exactly the balance on my cards.

As of today, my balance on my PayPal virtual credit card is $1,823 and my main credit card is $6,987.84. But I just bought some SKIMS bras because I had a thirty percent off coupon that was too good to pass up, so please add $70 to that total. It's safe to assume I have just short of $10,000 in credit card debt. Although this is certainly not a down payment on an apartment in 2026 Los Angeles, it is not an insignificant amount of money to have spent mainly on vintage designer clothing. Even if every piece was a really good deal.

My numbers are much lower than the national average

and lower than ten percent of my income, and overall has not at this point affected me too badly. But my numbers are still too damn high for frivolous spending and I know that.

I never set out to accumulate a bunch of debt. My first designer pieces I saved up for, but over time I started buying more, thinking I would pay them off later. A tale as old as time, I didn't, and then I got to where I am now. A girl with a pound of debt but with many one-of-a-kind runway pieces hanging in her closet in her studio apartment.

Sex and the City often faces criticism for depicting an unrealistic lifestyle, especially when it comes to Carrie and her clothes and restaurant spending. She was seemingly always out on the town wearing a new outfit on the budget of a writer who writes one column a week. The show, however, never shied away from the fact that Carrie was putting the bulk of her designer clothing on credit cards. Buzzfeed estimates Carrie's credit card debt to have hit an estimated one million.[3] I don't think the writers of the show were exactly running the numbers, but I do think we are meant to believe Carrie was indeed in a lot of debt.

Carrie's credit card use was so imprudent throughout the series, I would argue that it is the show itself that normalized debt for me. In a way Carrie having a credit card was an extension of the show's feminist messaging, as women in the United States could not get credit cards in their own name until 1974. The show depicted Carrie and her friends as independent not only from men sexually but financially. But Carrie was emotionally and romantically reckless, so her financial recklessness seemed to be a normal part of her character.

I am going to be honest: I don't think credit cards are bad. I think having them is necessary and not using them slightly beyond your means is a great sin, so I consider them a moral neutral. I want women to invest more, to get paid the same as men, and excel in a society where the deck is stacked against us. But I am not a writer who can easily tell my reader that all debt is bad and they should learn from me and my mistakes and not start charging things.

There is a lot I could not have done in this life without credit cards. There are a lot of things that lead to me getting more money I couldn't have done without credit cards. My first credit card purchase and the reason I got a credit card in the first place, was a Best Buy credit card (one I paid off and no longer have) where I purchased my first Mac book (very Carrie Bradshaw) on which I wrote my first satirical articles and eventual essays, the first pieces of writing I ever got paid for. It was the credit card that allowed me to become a writer.

Credit cards have allowed me to travel both as a stand-up comedian and as a writer that have led to more job opportunities. They have allowed me to create the experiences I will write or joke about later and they have allowed me access into rooms desperately needed into even if I couldn't afford it. I've put educational courses on credit cards that finally gave me the knowledge and the tools to make money doing what I love. I've put cocktails on credit that I've sipped during conversations that brought thousands of dollars worth of work. When I think back, I cannot help but be fundamentally pro-credit card.

I also believe that we've created a world where debt is classy for the rich, who we assume are investing in themselves and therefore the economy and society at large, but trashy for the poor who we assume are frivolous and bad with money. As a high-low girl, I am proud to say I am both: frivolous and investing in my future. In *Sex and the City* we see this in both Carrie and Charlotte who manifested the lives they wanted through means they at first did not have: Carrie through debt and Charlotte through marriage and then ultimately divorce. Both created an image that attracted the parts of their lives they felt were missing be it personal, professional, or real estate. It is ultimately this understanding of image creation that led to the tension in their relationship when Charlotte did not immediately offer Carrie the money for her down payment. It is only when Carrie reminds Charlotte of how she got her own apartment that she offers up the funds to her friend.

As an icebreaker at my thirty-third birthday party, my friends, many of them writers and artists, all confessed how much credit card debt they were in. The answers varied but I found that my number was around the normal amount to the lower end.

The biggest contributor to our combined debts seemed to be the same things: periods of unemployment in expensive cities, book tours and promotions that we did not get the anticipated returns on, and, of course, clothing. Almost all of us, working writers, felt at least in some way that how we dressed was an extension of what we put on the page, an extension of our literary personas.

Although many of my first credit card purchases were investments in my career, I can admit they eventually expanded to fashion. But what can I say - I am also a sucker for the history of the well-dressed writer. The history of the writer with a signature style goes back much further than *Sex and the City* and is almost synonymous with the persona of the author. We think of Joan Didion's sunglasses or Fran Lebowitz's suit jackets, or Truman Capote's WASPy sensibilities. Good writers have always had style.

In a famous quote attributed to Oscar Wilde, the notably well-dressed writer quips, "Anyone who lives within their means suffers from a lack of imagination," a seemingly commentary on the writer as a dreamer and above the social classes assigned to them. Wilde was known for having many debts that he could not pay.

In her 2021 piece for Elle, "The Irony of Writers Who Dress Well," Lauren Stroh writes of her nostalgia for the era of the well-dressed writer noting, "Fashion and writing, though distinct and separate industries, often find themselves intertwined, even married." Writers have often formed personas based not only on personality quirks but how they dress.[4]

Unfortunately the industry has changed and the age of the well-dressed writer is no longer possible. Like Carrie, I am just a girl who has fallen into the glorious, but expensive, trap of the well-dressed writer/party girl hybrid putting my work uniform (something designer as well as fashionable) on credit. It is a prison but a common one at least.

Stroh goes on to point out a paradoxical truth: "Under capitalism and in a society as materialistic as America, so much of our personal branding influences the way we are perceived by the outside world. The way we adorn ourselves reflects both the current material conditions of our lives and the future lives we aspire to lead. But because writers' wardrobes are increasingly subsidized outside of their writing instead of because of it, those who dress best mislead readers about the realities of working in an industry in rapid decline. Therein lies the paradox."[5]

I feel this paradox every time I open Instagram and see many of my friends and myself attending reading parties and other book events dressed to the nines in clothing we probably cannot afford. The same paradox is especially true when the conversation at such events turns to our declining industry and how many of us work multiple jobs in order to just live and write, not to mention dress the part.

I can say that the outfit I wore to the launch of my first book in 2024, cost more than the money I made on the book itself. Perhaps not only for me but for my peers, there is some self-actualization in the choice of dress. *I'm not a boring office worker, I'm a writer,* we think when we zip up our three hundred dollar, way-too chunky-for-the-office leather boots. Dress for the job you want to have, or the one you have but doesn't quite pay your bills.

Because writing and fashion are still at least somewhat married forms of culture, many writers I know are champions of independent designers. The designer Tyler McGillivary, is, in my opinion, the literary "it girl's" designer. McGillivary is championed by Caroline Calloway, the woman behind *Polyester Zine*, along with other writers within the New York City and London media scenes. Most of the pieces in McGillivary's collections start at around two hundred dollars, but because I love the looks, and perhaps because of my desire to dress the part, I own many of the designer's pieces and have worn them to numerous literary events. When I see a McGillivary piece in the world, I usually assume that the person wearing it is at least in some sense a writer, and so the self-actualization on behalf of the wearer becomes reality for the right audience.

I currently only own two plates and can see three designer pieces from where I'm sitting in my studio apartment. I'm not sad about it; I can eat out of old lo mein take-out containers. This is a financial choice I made, but in order to live the life I want and cultivate the persona to go along with it, a necessary one.

Along with my killer, although I will admit, excessive wardrobe, credit cards have allowed me to expand my skills and education as a writer, travel to places my ancestors could never have dreamed of, and allowed me to pursue opportunities that opened doors to my continued success. These open doors have also led to a bigger world for me to experience and explore, and therefore write about. Without my line of credit, I would not be the person or the writer I am or have the career I have today.

I can say for certain Carrie is the reason I have credit card debt. If it wasn't for her I would not be brave enough to have it. It is weird to think that getting oneself in massive amounts of debt is an act of bravery for me, at least to a certain extent it is. Seeing a single girl bet on herself and pay for what she wanted with a credit card is an act of bravery. Because charging something that you assume your future self will be able to pay for is a bet on oneself. Or in Carrie's case, a bet on a handsome investment banker who's been emotionally abusing you for a decade to pay it off. Carrie hedged her bets in the right direction even if it took decades and I am hoping the same will be true for me and my true love, art.

As a writer I cannot help but also feel like the way I dress is a form of self-actualization. Like Carrie, I dress therefore I am. I'm not a boring office worker, I'm a writer. I am a writer and this, *this*, is all for the story, not for the check.

I was at a book launch when a fellow writer and friend teasingly pointed out what should have been obvious to me for some time: "Oh, you have a shopping addiction."

At the time, I was very offended. I wouldn't have said "addiction." I would have said "bad habit." But then I finally realized my recoil and defensiveness means it's probably an addiction. That being said, I really don't want to be called a shopping addict in the same way someone who is already drunk at brunch doesn't want to be called an alcoholic, even if it is only ten in the morning. I shop because it feels good. I shop because I enjoy the rush it sends to my brain. Addiction is probably the right word. Maybe.

It feels good to feel pretty. It feels good to feel like you are part of a social or economic class you are not. It feels good to get to wear pieces of art. I've been drunk many times, I've done some drugs. Both are fine, but it is nothing to the rush of opening a box and finding a designer garment wrapped in white paper. I like looking in my closet and seeing my collection staring back at me, and being able to say *this is me, this is who I am*. I am the girl with the good clothes.

I may not have the funds, but the ability to create my own identity, one that expresses who I am on the inside and how I want to project to the world, and therefore signal how they should treat and approach me, is worth every penny.

Don't treat me like the girl who has to work a nine to five

as an executive assistant, treat me as the author I really am. In return, I'll make sure I always dress the part, so you won't get confused.

Like Carrie Bradshaw famously said, "I like my money where I can see it, hanging in my closet."[6]

Throughout *Sex and the City*, we see Carrie chase the same high because that's what fashion does to us. We start chasing the rush of a new outfit. And then the ones we've worn already don't feel as good. The cycle of needing more and more begins and then a true addiction emerges, which is unfortunately now what I can say happened to me. The cycle of catching up with the other cool girl writers and the cycle of trying to heal my inner demons.

"So here I was, a 35 year old single woman with no financial security but many life experiences behind me," Carrie muses as she still tries to find the money for her apartment.[7]

Each of my designer pieces are an experience to me. They represent something I found and studied and loved and offered a little bit of fleeting happiness in a very dark time in my history. Joy is so rare in this world that I cannot be too mad at myself.

My experience with credit cards started out innocently enough. That first Moschino felt better than anything. I would go on to chase that high again and again. Not realizing that I was acting as destructive as if I were drinking or doing drugs.

It's just a little debt. And then a little turned into a little more and a little more. As I write out every part of the pleasure I get from the experience, I am actually surprised my bill is not higher.

When I would look at my credit card statement, I would

think of Carrie and her nonchalant outlook on her own credit card debt. Something that was there but that she never really lost sleep over. She never considered it a deterrent in finding a partner. I think on some level she thought the expensive clothes would lead to a quality partner. I am confident if we were to ask Carrie she would spew off in her column some bullshit that justified her debt. Something like, *I couldn't help but wonder, was investing in a quality wardrobe investing in a quality love life?*

Carrie only dated rich guys. Maybe we are meant to assure they would clear her debt. Find a man, find someone to pay the Visa bill in full. It is not a very feminist message, but it seems like if you count the spinoff films and reboot, that's exactly what happened. The Cut even remarked in regard to *And Just Like That*, the reboot of *Sex and the City*, in a 2024 headline "When Did Carrie Bradshaw Get So Damn Rich?"[8]

I am sure there is some truth to that scenario. It is harder to get some investment banker to be in an on-again and off-again toxic relationship with you when you are rocking Target rather than Chanel. Clothes are class signifiers, and it is easier to date up when you look the part. It is also much more likely you will get into a room where your Mr. Big might be sitting at the bar when you have the proper clothes. Clothes can be an investment, if you wear them wisely.

For me, a cocktail of body trauma, and an aspirational lifestyle based on a career and economy that no longer really exists, created an almost ten thousand dollar deficit. I am willing to forgive myself for the former. The latter is some dumb shit I still participate in and I know hating myself isn't going to help. But I am hoping that I can find a way to remind myself not to be dumb and stop overspending. After all, I am not really attracted to investment bankers so I cannot follow in Carrie's footsteps.

My family hates debt. We talk about it a lot and I pretend that I don't have it. My grandma once asked me how much and I said, "oh, some." When she brings it up, I deflect the conversation. My grandma knows my number of sexual partners and the time I got so high I nearly broke my own pelvic floor because I kept trying to pee when I didn't have to. But my debt, I hide from her. It would cause her stress. Bad finances have very real repercussions and they are trying to protect me from that.

I am going to try to do better. I am putting these words into print and my mom yelling at me (or since I am an adult, being disappointed in doing a bad job teaching me about money) is way scarier than any compound interest will ever be. If I know myself, and I do, I will probably spend the next year before this book is published paying down my card in anticipation of whatever conversation we may have. I suppose I am including it in this book because I want her to.

But I can't promise I am going to quit shopping. I like it so much and an addict has to want to quit.

As I age, I realize that I need to figure out my finances and that being the single girl who buys designer clothes on credit instead of replacing her sagging mattress must come to an end. It is time. Or more importantly, it is down payment time, because I need to find a stable place to house my vast collection. Unfortunately, I do not have a Charlotte or even a Mr. Big in my life who can loan me an interest-free forty thousand dollars.

But at least, like Carrie, I currently know where my money is: "hanging in my closet."

I WANT A MAN WITH A SLUTTY NECK

This book almost didn't get written because I developed a porn addiction. To be more accurate, since I prefer to read about sex than watch strangers have it, I guess the proper term is a *smut addiction*.

"Smut" is a slang term for literature with sexual content, also known as erotica. Although according to a quick Google search I did on the difference, erotica is supposed to contain actual plot. Reading either regularly can still be considered a form of porn addiction, which to me feels dramatic. The images I come up with in my head do not exploit or damage a real person. Nor am I even usually imagining a real person, but instead a fictional being, who won't have to face any real social or economic consequences.

Because I am nothing if not predictable, when writing a book about my pop culture obsessions, I also developed… another pop culture obsession. What I did not expect was to become someone who constantly had to hide that she was reading a story involving Regency era aristocrats fingering each other under a weeping willow. On her phone while in the elevator at her office job.

At thirty-two, I had to tell one of my more than gracious editors that I was not meeting any of my writing deadlines because I could not stop reading fanfiction inspired by Netflix's Regency era show *Bridgerton*.

Fanfiction is a genre of internet-based writing where fans

create new or reimagined storylines involving characters from their favorite forms of media, usually television or fantasy novels. In the case of *Bridgerton*, which is a television show based on a series of novels, the related fanfiction will often pull inspiration from both of the book and show canons.

Fanfiction allows devotees to veer away from the original canon of an imagined universe and allows the writer to create fantasy worlds all their own, but without having to establish and develop new characters and instead use ones they already feel connected to. *Fifty Shades of Grey*, which became a series of romance novels and feature films that explore BDSM, started out as fanfiction based on the *Twilight* books.

Fanfiction is known for being incredibly sexual as an overall genre, and erotic scenes involving fans' favorite characters is par for the course. This is especially true for the *Bridgerton* fanfiction universe, considering the original material in the fantasy romance genre contains many intimate scenes, and the television show's cast is full of incredibly conventionally attractive actors. I currently have one hundred and thirteen *Bridgerton* fanfictions bookmarked on my Archive of my Own account, the website where I read and write fanfiction. Of those, at least one hundred are rated "mature" or "explicit," meaning they contain some degree of sexual content. Although I enjoy the shows, it's safe to say I'm not just reading it for a scene where the *Bridgerton* brothers partake in another round of fencing.

As a writing instructor, I teach a workshop entitled "Writer as Obsessive, Writing the Pop Culture Essay." As I tell my students, I developed the class because I understand obsession. Waves of hyperfixation on pieces of media have consumed me since childhood. I have developed many obsessions over the course of my life, all for various purposes and reasons, and all because of some type of avoidance. I will obsess over a movie, rare painting, or little known television show in order to avoid doing something else - be it a necessary break-up, filing taxes, or finally figuring out why I've had the same awful cough for three years until eventually I have trouble breathing nearly every day. Luckily, I am still a somewhat reasonable adult and I will, eventually, put down my obsession of the day, week, or year and go find a doctor that will diagnose me with adult onset asthma.

It makes sense that as I wrote this book, which was a scary undertaking, I developed an obsession to avoid, well, writing this book. I assume if you are reading this, I was able to defeat my biggest enemy (me) and get something over to my publisher.

In 2024 while still trying to write this book, I watched *Bridgerton* season three when it premiered after having enjoyed the two previous seasons. A day later, I watched season three again at my friend Greg's perfectly decorated apartment after we ate some truly mediocre Mediterranean food. I pretended I was watching it for the first time, even though I had cheated and totally watched it the moment it dropped the night before. Then I walked back to my own apartment after leaving Greg's, turned it back on, and fell asleep. The next morning, I woke up and I turned it on again, watching the same episodes over and over again on a loop.

I liked living in the *Bridgerton* world. Because it takes place in Regency England, it feels complicated in a way that is controlled and understood. Shonda Rhimes, *Bridgerton*'s executive producer, excels at drama that is both high stakes and somehow still relaxing for the viewer; it is a cocktail she has mastered and the world is better for it. I love Shonda so much, my lime tree is named Shonda Limes.

Like the books, each season of *Bridgerton* focuses on one of the eight *Bridgerton* siblings finding love. Each season is based on a traditional romance trope (i.e., fake dating, enemies to lovers, love triangle). Season three of *Bridgerton* is a friends-to-lovers plot and is unique in that the central couple of the season, Colin and Penelope, have been part of the ensemble cast since season one and therefore have a much longer backstory. Because of this, the lead characters have greater shared history than previous couples, allowing for a deeper emotional intimacy. As a viewer, this intimacy is very satisfying to see on screen.

Several days later, I still hadn't stopped. I watched Colin and Penelope's love story over and over again. I downloaded the Netflix app on my phone and played it through my headphones at my office job while I managed my bosses' calendars and negotiated vendor contracts. Then I would go home and watch it some more - I couldn't find it in myself to turn it off. When I had it on, my nervous system felt calm, my worries about hating my job or being skinny or lovable melted away to the sounds of the *Bridgerton* universe.

Penelope Featherington (Nicola Coughlan), the female lead of season three, is one of my favorite characters to ever grace my television. She is the eventual love of the third *Bridgerton* brother Colin (Luke Newton), as well as Lady Whistledown, the anonymous and powerful gossip writer that dominates the Ton. As a character, she is very easy to connect to as the shy overlooked wallflower, who according to the *Bridgerton* universe is "two stone heavier than she ought to be,"[1] and is secretly in love with a man she feels is out of her league romantically. In her story, we get the satisfaction of seeing the man she has secretly loved for two seasons fall in love with her and for the first time since maybe *Hairspray*, a story where "the big girl[*]" who has a secret talent gets the charming but insecure man she wants. (*Hairspray* and *Bridgerton* season three have so many cinematic parallels that the former's influence on the latter seems painfully obvious)[†] Only in *Bridgerton*, we finally get sex scenes between a regular-sized woman and the chiseled sought after man she adores.

For a lot of *Bridgerton* fanfiction, Penelope serves as the self insert for the female writer or reader. The character is perfect for audience projection as both overlooked wallflower and remarkable woman of words. It would make sense that women who express themselves through fanfiction would feel a kinship with her as we are both creating our own stories, but have to because our real lives are lacking in some way that compels us to write fantasy in the first place.

Because *Bridgerton* is set in Regency era England, the men are almost always wearing cravats and therefore have their necks covered completely. Unless one of them loosens it or

---

[*] Despite being repeatedly referred to as "plus sized" in the press surrounding season three, Nicola was a size ten during filming.[2]

[†] A fat girl who is the best at something in her town loves a popular and desirable man. She is socially ostracized for calling out the injustice of the society she lives in and then it all comes to a climax at one big final dance where the town and the man she loves finally embrace her for her talents.

takes it off, and becomes what I saw someone online call "a little neck slut," and bare their uncovered throat. If you want to make a body part very alluring, cover up that body part, so through the show's cravats, I learned that the male neck can become deeply erotic. After watching the show, I suddenly found myself noticing men's necks and fantasizing about licking their Adam's apples.

When I could not actively be watching television, I would look at Twitter, (all while feeling slightly bad that I was spending time on an app owned by a fascist) whose algorithm was quick to feed me many tweets about the new *Bridgerton* season. I liked scrolling my Twitter feed and seeing fans swoon over Penelope and Colin's best moments and scenes. As it fed me more *Bridgerton* fan content, it eventually started showing me something I had not explored since I was a teen: fanfiction.

I had read some fanfiction in high school, mostly of the Green Day or My Chemical Romance variety. Back then, I was a bored virgin who enjoyed reading works written by other bored virgins. Most of what I read involved my favorite band members taking a teenage female self insert character with them on global tours or to award shows and they did lots of missionary with heavy eye contact.

One day after I read an intriguing sneak peak of someone's story on Twitter, I couldn't resist the temptation to check it out. I felt incredibly silly as I pulled up Archive of Our Own at thirty-two. I was already a published writer with a mile long list of talented friends' books left unread and not enough hours in the day to catch up. Why was I going to waste my reading time on what were probably bored teenagers inserting themselves into a Romantasy world? To my surprise, what I found wasn't written by teenagers. Instead I found *Bridgerton*-inspired stories and incredibly well-written scenes crafted expertly by not only adults, but seemingly sophisticated and articulate women.

After a few too many weeks than I am willing to admit, I did turn off the television. The obsession had served its purpose of thoroughly distracting me from my day-to-day life and writing this book for just the right amount of time. What stayed in my routine, however, was fanfiction.

If I thought watching the television show was time consuming, reading fanfiction was worse. Immediately I couldn't get enough, I had never read adult women write about the sex they wanted, the sex they dreamed of so unfiltered. Once I started, I couldn't look away. I found myself updating the *Bridgerton* tag every couple of hours just to see if anyone had written anything new I could read between Zoom meetings. Despite my huge stack of unread books at home, I somehow found that over the course of a single day, I could easily read hundreds of thousands of words of emotional, but deeply graphic, descriptions of sexual acts and kinks I'd never heard of. Turns out you can get a lot done if what you're doing makes you constantly horny.

I had read some traditional erotica before, but what I was finding in fanfiction felt different; it was so honest and personal, a peek into someone else's deepest fantasies, not filtered through the lens of traditional media. I wanted to see what other women were wanting, what they desired, what I could desire. A female gaze emerged throughout my reading that I realized I was unfamiliar with. I learned about things I didn't know I could want. Although the stories I was reading were primarily about Colin and Penelope, their story became less interesting to me as I focused on the subtext of the fics, the rarely expressed sexual and romantic yearnings of women.

Things were happening in fanfictions that I never considered. First, because fanfiction is primarily written by women, the women come. *They come a lot.* Men always take time to make women come before penetration, usually through fingering, but sometimes through oral or oftentimes both. Which I realized, and felt rather embarrassed about, makes sense. Considering it is nearly impossible to come from penetration alone, why aren't all straight men making sure there is already one orgasm on the scoreboard before inserting themselves into the game? It is common in fanfiction for a male character to "not allow" the woman access to his dick until she has "given him at least two." It was something I had never considered and then seemed so entirely obvious.

A few months into my fanfiction obsession, I started dating a new guy and brought up this revelation to him. "I never thought that a man should make me come once before penetration, that just makes way more sense."

"Of course that's how it should be, you should come multiple times, as a woman you can come multiple times, why would I not want you to come multiple times?" he replied as if it was the most obvious thing in the world and I had been having sex incorrectly my entire life.

A few dates later, we had sex for the first time. He did not even attempt to make me come by any means before trying to penetrate me. When I left his room, only one person had finished, and it wasn't me.

In fanfiction, penetration is slow to be introduced and worked up to, or perhaps removed entirely. The male characters delay wanting to finish because they want the encounter to last as long as possible.

In *Pornography: Men Possessing Women*, Andrea Dworkin argues pornography is from the symbolic point of view of that of the male penis. Therefore male wants and desires consume the entire encounter, leaving little room for an equal exchange of pleasure. I would agree that in traditional heterosexual porn, as we watch the main character (the dick), the viewer takes on its wants and desires neglecting female pleasure. In fanfiction, the point of view is often third person and focuses on a previously developed or developing relationship between characters the reader is already emotionally invested in. As readers, we want the equal exchange of pleasure, for the sexual encounter to be a scene in which a conversation happens, because we are invested in the characters' interior lives. Other times the point of view is of the writer themselves as the self insert and readers then take on their wants and desires, both sexual and emotional.[3] Regardless of the point of view, in fanfiction the dick is never the focus nor narrator.

I spent many of my past sexual experiences with men waiting for them to be over. I enjoyed getting to the bedroom way more than I liked what was happening in it. I like kissing a lot, I like skin to skin contact with another warm body, especially if I feel tender emotions towards the person that body belongs to, and I like the validation of someone wanting to have sex with me. I don't really enjoy fucking men, at least not past the first - let's give it a generous - ninety seconds. After about a minute and a half in, I'm bored. I also know immediately if I'm going to finish (probably not), so I am mostly waiting it out.

I read an internet meme once that says if a girl asks a man to come, she's bored. I can attest to that being 100 percent true. Over the course of my life I have whispered the words "Come for me baby," into at least a half a dozen ears, all because I wanted to get whatever man off me and return my attention back to where it belongs - on the television.

I came of age during the rise of internet porn, where pornography was seeping its way into mainstream media along with its gaze and camera angles. An era where porn began to influence many of our sexual experiences whether consciously or more often purposely. In my case, after my early sexual experiences were filled with intimate partner violence, any sex that was at least consensual I didn't examine too closely. Perhaps with my history of sexual abuse or my repressed queerness, when it came to desire, I felt completely lost. I felt extremely horny, but I wasn't exactly sure what *for*.

All I knew was that I was so tired of having sex where it felt like another person was masturbating with my body rather than trying to connect and feel pleasure *with* me. Tired after years of lackluster or harmful sex and even more lackluster or harmful relationships with men.

To see the type of sex people were writing about in fanfiction was revolutionary to me. I had never seen descriptions of sex where two people were not only physically but also emotionally and spiritually engaged in a way that didn't feel staged. Where characters communicated their wants and desires openly and the other party worked to make sure those desires were met. I had never read descriptions where one partner got pleasure purely from another partner's pleasure and not just their own. I realized I had yet to understand my own desires or develop my own sensuality. I didn't know what I wanted, and suddenly I was discovering an internet black hole of endless possibilities.

In her Tedx talk, *It's Time for Porn to Change*, the filmmaker Erika Lust recalls her revelation about pornography "Porn isn't just porn. Porn is actually a discourse, a discourse about sexuality, about masculinity, about femininity, and the roles we play," she goes on to say, "...I realized that the only ones participating in the discourse of pornography are men - chauvinistic men, narrow-minded men..."[4]

In fanfiction women are speaking about what they want from sex. They are participating in the discourse. Finally I was able to hear other voices and understand other ways of not only having sex, but thinking about it. Erika Lust wants to get women into porn. Fanfiction may not be the same as working behind the camera, but it's another way of expressing our sexual point of view.

In each season of *Bridgerton*, we follow the season's new lead characters through different but similar emotional arcs, overcoming some external and societal, but mostly internal obstacles, in order to live in harmony with their true love. They battle childhood trauma, feelings of inadequacy, and their own stubbornness along with Regency era social norms. At its root *Bridgerton* is about battling inner demons so you can experience true intimacy. Because it is a fantasy, *Bridgerton* also puts incredibly sexy men in Regency era dress and gives them the emotional journeys of twentieth century men who have experienced massive amounts of therapy and self-reflection.

Because of the emotional journeys the *Bridgerton* characters embark on, its fanfiction frequently explores not only sex, but emotional intimacy, vulnerability, and affection between the couples. Along with sexual desires I have never encountered, I became equally interested in the romantic desires that fanfiction writers would include in their work. The male characters are doting and attentive to their partners' emotional needs. They always know what gifts to buy. They remember important anniversaries and celebrate them. They already are or become excellent, present fathers. They actually care about the women they have sex with as people and recognize their needs.

Most interesting (and mindblowing) to me were the fics that included some type of aftercare ritual, as I didn't really know what aftercare was. I started looking for #aftercare as an additional tag within the *Bridgerton* fanfiction universe. I was fascinated by the male characters who were still as attentive after sex as they were during or before. They bathe their partners, feed them, or rub ointment on their freshly spanked rear ends. I spent hours reading about different forms of aftercare realizing that sex didn't have to end once the man finished, but was supposed to have an entire third act with things as simple as water and cuddles or more elaborate gestures like bubble baths and massages. I was particularly tickled by a writer's modern version of an Anthony Bridgerton who threw towels in the dryer before lovemaking so he could wrap his wife in warmth as part of a postcoital shower routine.

While learning about aftercare, I felt icky remembering a time with my long-term boyfriend, where after he finished he got up from our bed, pulled out from inside me without a word, and went to take piss with the door open only stopping to change the music on his phone to heavy metal. The sexual experience was over for him, so it was over for me. At that moment I was upset, but didn't say anything, because I didn't know what to say. He wouldn't have been able to get hard again, so I wasn't sure what to ask from him.

In episode four of season three of *Bridgerton*, Colin tenderly rights Penelope's disheveled dress and hair after they have a steamy encounter in a carriage. Penelope, unfamiliar with someone caring for her, watches as Colin takes his time putting her sleeve back and brushing a loose curl behind her ear. "What are you doing?" she asks as he fixes her.[5] She is able to see his intention in his actions, to make her presentable and hide the evidence of their tryst, but she is unfamiliar with being tended to. I found the scene deeply satisfying, knowing I would have a similar reaction to this small act of care. This scene is often repeated and expanded in fanfiction as a subtle form of doting - that feels radical coming from a man.

We tell women when they are looking for a partner to make sure they have standards, but we never really say what those standards should be. We are told not to settle but that life is not a fairy tale and to be realistic in what we want from a relationship. Where does one see these so-called realistic standards so we can have them? When a fantasy scene with a straightening of a sleeve and the tucking of a curl feels revolutionary, what can we really reasonably expect from men in real life?

Growing up, many of the adult men in my life did not seem like the type of partner I would want to have one day. They monopolized conversations without letting anyone else get a word in, they didn't help mop the floor, they didn't always remember Valentine's Day, they went fishing even if there was an important event they would miss. I can think of many times when I would ask an older woman in my life why they allowed the men to act that way.

"One day you will have a husband that does the same," was the answer I usually got, "Men are just like that, they are selfish."

It amazed me that it was already decided for me by those I loved the most that I would end up with someone who wasn't caring or thoughtful or considerate. That was the story that was being told to me. I didn't look for a man who was caring or doting because I was never told that I should.

As fanfiction broadened my sexual desires, it did the same for my intimate and emotional expectations. I had always thought I knew what I wanted in a partner: someone kind, ambitious, and well read. But suddenly I was exposed to many other qualities I hadn't considered - like being considerate or willing to stick up for me or attentive enough to realize when I was uncomfortable. That I could want someone to take on some of the load in life. These are qualities I now realize I should have been looking for all along and was lacking in my previous relationships - I just didn't know I was supposed to be searching for them.

I started to find it slightly ironic that I was unable to realize what I wanted for myself in a relationship is to be treated the way myself and many other women have always treated our male partners. When I'm with a man, I give head rubs, I stay up all night making cinnamon rolls, I have snacks delivered to their job when they have a long night, I notice when their shoulders tense up, I can sense when they want to leave a party. But in my twenties I didn't have the capacity to want this level of care for myself because I'd never seen it depicted in media or in real life. I didn't realize I could want to be cared for in a nurturing way the same way I care for them.

The men in fanfiction wake up their partners with kisses or cups of tea or cunnilingus. They wash their lovers' hair. They never let them come less than twice at minimum. They pack their lunch for work. They know what to do with their fingers. They ask follow-up questions about their partner's day. They don't have to be reminded to take out the garbage. They already took care of the house and the kids - oh, and they baked muffins.

The men in fanfiction have amazing sex because they are amazing lovers. They understand that desire and arousal are connected to care and intimacy. They know killer blowjobs are more comfortably given on a freshly cleaned carpet from a stress-free wife, so they already went ahead and called the steamer company.

"What do you like?" is a question I have been asked by various men in real life as well as seen asked of women in media repeatedly (including *Bridgerton* season one). What I see less is women knowing how to answer that question, because we are rarely shown options of things we might actually like, sexual or emotional. When I was asked this same question, I would say things like "more" but not exactly know what more means. In *Bridgerton* season one when the Duke asks Daphne what she likes in bed she says, "you."[6] It's hard to know what you want when you've only been presented with a tiny amount of the options, so you do your best to answer with the limited information you have.

I know there is a lot of talk about how nearly impossible to find an interesting and emotionally intelligent man to date. As someone with an active Raya and Hinge account, I can attest this is unfortunately very true. The men available seem to either be Joe Rogan enthusiasts, MAGA republicans, performative male feminists who still treat women shitty, carnivores who think fiber is a myth, plain old regular chauvinists, or unaware that human beings are supposed to brush their teeth more than once a month. It's hard out there, but I discovered I was so focused on avoiding these types of landmines when dating that I never even considered what I actually wanted and was willing to accept the bare minimum.

For so long I didn't know I was allowed to have intimate and emotional desires that I am having trouble figuring out exactly what mine are. Luckily I now have been exposed to many options. I am not a particularly tidy person, but I have heard many women state that they simply want a clean house, that a man taking on some part of the housework is sexy to them. That having someone take on some of the housework meets their emotional needs. How a partner taking care of the domestic labor could create a sense of comfort allowing for more room for arousal is not a hard leap for me, but it is still something that most straight men cannot seem to connect.

As a genre, romance is often criticized as unrealistic when depicting relationships. The love stories in the genre are supposed to be fantasies, partly because of the way straight male characters act. I wouldn't say everything presented in the romance genre is "unrealistic," but I would use the word "aspirational." I would use it in the same context that someone wants to make money as an influencer or sell a screenplay. Aspirational as in not impossible, but it will take both work and an incredible amount of luck. It also takes finding someone willing to play the part - slutty little neck cravat optional.

Instead of thinking of the sex and care I found in fanfiction as fantasy, I started seeing it as a menu. What *could* I ask for in real life? What was in the words I couldn't stop reading that I could bring into my real life? What was actually possible? I didn't want to spend hours a day slipping into a mythical world. I wanted to pull as much as I could from that mythical world into my reality.

"The bar is on the floor" is a statement I hear often from women in regards to straight men. With a little help from fanfiction fantasy land, I was able to pick up my bar and move it much closer to where it should have been all along. Because I never realized where exactly the bar should be until I started reading about what the ceiling might look like. I was finally getting a lesson on extremes that were moving my bare minimum higher than it'd ever been before.

Since I don't always orgasm when dating men, I have always masturbated in front of my partners, a piece of advice I got from sex writer Dan Savage, who would frequently tell callers on his podcast something along the lines of: if your partner doesn't know how to touch you, show them how you like to be touched. Unfortunately some of the men I have done this in front of, instead of taking the well-presented learning opportunity with a willing and very present coach, have at some point made a comment about how boring it is to watch me masturbate. As if I want to be doing it alone.

The men of fanfiction are paying close attention. If a woman masturbates in front of them, they grow glasses and a legal pad and are taking detailed notes on rhythm and pressure. They care deeply about their partner's pleasure, because they care, and because they get pleasure from their partner's pleasure. As I read, I suddenly realized how bizarre it is that you can be so close and intimate with another person - being sexual with them - and also completely ignore them. I realized how often I was having sex with people who were doing just that. I uncovered just how bad things were in my relationships by reading about good ones.

In fanfiction characters go above and beyond to pleasure each other. Characters take time to learn about each other and their desires. They worship each other's bodies, are turned on by their partner's every imperfection, and understand their every facial expression. They can make each other finish a million different ways. I won't go as far to say this is something that is completely impossible but something incredibly rare that requires not only commitment but time, as well as the right partner.

More than anything, I was disappointed to learn how little me and my previous partners had been communicating. I was under the impression that after my assault, I was good at communicating not only enthusiastic consent, but also my wishes. Although I do think that's true, I realize now I was only communicating consent and my wishes that I felt didn't inconvenience or ask too much of my partners. I was so happy to be having nonviolent and consensual sex, I didn't push for deeply satisfying sex. I now know that it is okay to ask and to expect more than just someone who makes sure I consent, but also someone who makes sure I am getting pleasure. I know now I can want a generous lover.

One line not from *Bridgerton* the television show, but from Julia Quinn's original novel about Colin and Penelope, *Romancing Mister Bridgerton,* shows up frequently in fanfiction: "A kiss is for two people,"[7] Colin says to Penelope when they first share a snog in the drawing room. Penelope is hesitant at first, so Colin encourages her exploration and participation in their intimate moment. At first, I didn't notice much when the line showed up repeatedly. Throwing in a few lines from the original canon is a large part of fanfiction. But then I realized how frequently I saw the line included.

It's a line about consent, but more than that. It's about connection, it's about the unspoken nuances when engaging in intimacy and giving them words. The romance in the line is Colin's focus that he and Penelope experience the kiss together. He is not just kissing her - they are kissing each other.

A kiss, or any sexual experience, is for two people.

In my first sexual relationship, the negotiations were not for two people. I was frequently met with the same line, one that enrages me for the younger version of myself and shocks me at its simplicity in coercion.

"But what if I would like that?"

When I would speak with my boyfriend at the time about sexual acts I wanted or did not want, he, a decade older than me, would often respond with with the same line.

"I do not want you to touch my head while I am giving a blow job," I would say.

"But what if I would like that?"

"I do not want to give you head while you stand. I would prefer it if you lay down."

"But what if I would like that?"

A few simple words that lead to a world of guilt and a subtle but progressive breakdown of my self-esteem and boundaries. In a few words, I was coerced into performing sex acts I didn't feel comfortable with and made to feel that I was not meeting his expectations of how a girlfriend should act. Slowly, over time, this led to more sexual and emotional coercions until there was very little I wouldn't do. In that world, sex was not for two people, but for the pleasure of one.

"A kiss is for two people," is a simple but almost radical line for many of us who have experienced sexual acts without explicit consent. Or in the same vein, had sex with someone who did not take the time to find a sexual rapport.

Because fanfiction loves the character to build sexual rapport, a large amount involves kink. I won't go too much into my own kinks, because my mom is going to read this essay even though I asked her not to, but I will say that as a child I have a VHS tape my grandma gave me where she taped the 1992 made-for-TV version of *Annie* (the one where Victor Garber plays Daddy Warbucks) not realizing she had also given me a VHS tape that included a late night showing of *Secretary*, a film that includes an aftercare routine, much to my delight.

Every year there is an online event that takes place where many *Bridgerton* fanfiction writers write kink pieces in the fall for something called "Polin Kinktober." During Polin (the nickname for the relationship between Penelope and Colin) Kinktober, writers create pieces of work in which the characters explore new or established kinks in an openly nonjudgmental, loving manner. They explore breastfeeding, anal play, cum play, stuff involving cat ears, and many other kinks including some that still manage to make me blush a little when I see them on my phone screen.

Although I am not interested in most of the kinks explored in these works, I liked reading about them, and I found that after reading a scene in which the characters try them out, I would be more open to some of them then I originally thought.

To my own delight and embarrassment, I was able to determine I have something I now know is called a praise kink. A praise kink is when a person gets pleasure or arousal from being praised or complimented. The most common phrase associated with the kink being "good girl" or some similar variation.

I have always known I want my partners to speak to me during sex but wasn't sure exactly what I wanted them to say. I then discovered that "you're being such a good girl for me" may be the most erotic sentence in the entire English language and the only reason I am choosing to include it in this essay is in the hopes that:

A) It will lose some of its power over me and I will no longer enjoy it as much as I do.
B) Someone who looks like Adam Driver will read this book and say it to me in the appropriate context (in a big hotel bed or on a sheepskin rug in front of a roaring fire).

When I first stumbled upon the Kinktober works, I discovered an author's subtitle of her Kinktober works that caught my attention and gave me pause:

"It's about being safe, trusted and loved…"[8]

Had I ever felt all three of those things at the same time during any sexual encounter? Had I ever felt both physically and emotionally safe enough to tell my partners everything I wanted to learn and explore, without judgment?

I have never thought of kink in this way before. Heck, I had never even thought of sex in this way before. It made me sad that something so simple, like safety and trust in the bedroom, was something I had never truly experienced. Even with my long-term partners, sexual exploration always came with hesitance, shame, or lack of curiosity and enthusiasm.

I've had a fair amount of partners, I've been in love more than once, I've lived with another person in what I thought at the time was a state of domestic bliss, but I've never had a period where I felt both emotionally and sexually fulfilled at the same time.

I want to feel safe, trusted (as well as trusting), and loved enough to have spectacular sexual experiences, but can't say I ever really have. And worse, I didn't even really notice what was missing because I don't think I'd seen much depiction in life or media of all these needs being met at once before. I started to understand kink in ways I have never thought about it before.[*]

I once read a piece of fanfiction where the characters do some shibari play that was so tender and had so much emotional trust and intimacy, I wept over my cell phone with my hands down my pants. I was so turned on but so sad I had

---

[*] If you are looking to read some of this I would suggest you start with the writer with the screen name ApplePuffSIlver. If you are wondering, no, that is not me, but damn I wish I was.

yet to experience that level of emotional and physical care with another human being.

In the midst of my fanfiction obsession, I went to dinner at El Coyote with my friend Tyler who revealed to me that at one point he had also developed a strong Archive of Our Own daily reading habit.

"Oh, I had to stop that," he bemoaned from our red vinyl booth. "My thoughts were getting so unrealistic and I knew I was never going to be able to meet a person that would hold up to that standard in real life."

This interested me because Tyler was someone who I knew had experimented with many kinks and seemed to be having great sex. At a previous point during the same dinner, we had been looking up ski masks because he was seeing a man who was interested in staged encounters of anonymous sex and Tyler was more than happy to make the fantasy a reality for him.

"You just won't ever find someone that you can have sex and intimacy with to that standard. The bar you end up setting is too high. I had to stop so I could experience real stuff in the world," he said as I flagged down our server for a refill on tortilla chips.

Although he did not tell me what fandom he was reading he did say it was an Archive of Our Own but nothing more, although I assume it was not Regency, straight, or of the Shonda Rhimes universe.

I explained to Tyler that I would argue that standards for men in romantic relationships are so low, it is worth creating a universe where they are exceptionally high. So I am choosing to take a very "shoot for the moon and end up among the stars" approach.

Tyler didn't seem convinced. I supposed he was right on one point: connection is not something you cannot ask for. It's something that has to develop or both parties have to choose. But care, attentiveness, and even a deep emotional connection is something you can look for - and that's better than nothing. I suppose buying a ski mask is a great start.

I, of course, do not think that there is someone out there with whom I will meet and then immediately start having mind-blowing multiple orgasms with, who will also fulfill all my romantic and emotional needs. But I do think if I am going to continue to date straight men I can start asking that they at least *try* to fulfill some of them, especially if I know what they are. Maybe they can figure out how to finger me correctly and keep some bubble bath I like at their house. At the very least I hope to no longer let the "men are just selfish" mentality keep me in unhappy relationships.

Just like how I was so focused on nonviolent sex that I was unable to push for great sex, the same can be said of my relationships. I was so happy to be having a nonabusive relationship, I was unable to dream about what a really good one would entail. Many works of fanfiction depict happy domestic relationships where male characters show up and support their female partners. They order or prepare food, spoil them with attention and various forms of pain relief during their periods, or take on the brunt of childcare without being asked. Emotional care is also featured regularly where male characters will defend their partners in front of rude family, undermining employers, or childhood bullies.

I couldn't get my ex to take my Kia through the car wash.

Of course, the part of the allure and the fantasy of the *Bridgerton* world is that it is filled with aristocrats who possess unlimited funds. And I would argue that the romance does set up unrealistic expectations for class in relationships and depict rich men as the only men worthy of desire. However, I will argue that paying attention to your partner and wanting them to have a great time in bed with you is free to all men.

I didn't realize how low my standards had become, how little I was willing to accept from partners - how much I had internalized "men are just like that" until I saw what others were able to desire and dream. But I was also starting to read so much of it when I should have been working on this book. I was pretty sure my editor was going to get on a plane and come kill me dead or, worse, send me a disappointed email.

It was a distraction, but I was also unlearning. Unlearning the male gaze, unlearning what I had convinced myself I liked because that was what boys liked, unlearning everything about relationships that *Everybody Loves Raymond* had taught me was hilarious and not utterly insane.

For so long I have been too focused on qualities in a romantic partner along the lines of "has a job," "doesn't vote for rapists," and "takes a shower" that I didn't have room to dream about things like, cares for me as deeply as I care for them. Or maybe even a little better.

As an bisexual woman, I've found myself becoming more and more interested in women as I aged, and was even considering not dating men anymore completely. So I was not expecting to develop an obsession that was so, well, straight. But I realized I wanted at least the option to have deeply emotional and sexually fulfilling passionate, romantic relationships with men as well as women.

I found myself both surprised and elated by the new desire I had for men. Maybe it was possible to have a relationship with a man that didn't leave me drained and lonely; I just hadn't seen it before nor knew how to look for it. This could turn out to be patriarchal propaganda rather than a form of healing, but I will say it feels good for now.

Regardless of my renewed interest, men do not have a good reputation right now. Men especially do not have good work histories nor can they provide many references when it comes to being fulfilling sexual and emotional partners, but I suddenly found myself filled with a burning desire for men with both visible back muscles and emotional intelligence who worship the ground I walk on and possess a sexy, lickable neck.

The more I read, the more obsessed I became with the author notes fanfiction writers would add at the ends of their works. Little notes like "sorry for a lack of updated chapters, my daughter was at camp when I started this fic," or "I am posting this in an Uber on the way to my husband's work party sorry for typos." These notes provided brief glimpses into their anonymous faceless authors' worlds. Of these faceless writers, many were married, many had babies, many alluded to being published writers and also only writing fics for fun. Many also noted being queer and not dating men in real life, but writing heterosexual fanfiction because they enjoyed the television show. Many fanfiction writers do not speak English as their first language and, as both a writing teacher and an American who is not bilingual, I am amazed at the works these writers come up with. The glimpses into the writer's lives intrigued me - these weren't teens or sad, lonely cat women making stuff up, these were a mix of women from various backgrounds exploring desire and writing out their fantasies. I am thankful to them for sharing as they have opened me up to desires I never knew I could have.

As I was working on this essay, I interviewed the writer Jamie Hood about her memoir *Trauma Plot, A Life* for a magazine article. Her memoir covers three decades of her life including multiple sexual assaults. The book's title comes from the term coined by Parul Sehgal in *The New Yorker* in which the critic compares stories of trauma to the classic marriage plot, "Unlike the marriage plot, the trauma plot does not direct our curiosity toward the future (*Will they or won't they?*) but back into the past (*What happened to her?*)."[9]

The *Bridgerton* books and, by extension, each individual season of the television show are all versions of the marriage plot. The *will they/won't they* always leads to marriage. Fan fiction pushes beyond this - it creates a what's next for the characters even when it is declared their story is finished.

As I was interviewing Hood, she expressed her want to move beyond the trauma plot in her own life and work. She told me about wanting more, more life and more sex and more pleasurable experiences. She wanted to create a life for herself where there was more to her story after assault. As she spoke I was so happy to hear another woman express what I also wanted for myself.[10]

About four months into to checking *#Bridgerton* multiple times a day, I bit the bullet and threw up the first chapter of my own *Bridgerton* fanfiction. I won't reveal my pen name, but I can say that the reception to my story was pretty good.

I was happy to practice asking for what I want, articulating my desires, so that in the future I would be more equipped to articulate them to a lover. Knowing my fantasies, so I can bring them into real life.

I get asked whenever I talk about fanfiction if I see the actors when I am reading or if I feel any particular connection to them. Although the physical character description in most fanfiction works do describe the *Bridgerton* actors, I do not really see their faces in my admittedly very horned-up brain. I may see their general outlines and maybe some version of the wig they were wearing. I see archetypes more than faces, as I have created a Colin and Penelope of my own. That being said, I do live in Hollywood. I would like to be able to look Luke Newton in the face without blushing if we ever make eye contact at a party.

I have been asked if I would ever explore outside of the *Bridgerton* universe when it comes to reading fanfiction. The answer is probably not; the *Bridgerton* world is simple in its tropes and characters, it allows for simplicity in plot and character development which allows writers, now including myself, to focus on deeper desires and messages within the prose. And like I said, I am now a slut for a man's bare neck.

Of course, *Bridgerton* is a fantasy world. The men in the Regency era would all be too busy being sexist and classist to carry me to the bed from the bath we just took together. I frequently remember that none of them would have owned deodorant. But I appreciate the window into a more emotionally and sexually fulfilling world, and I'm thankful for what it has opened up in my brain.

Finally, I feel like I know what I want and so I can speak

up and ask for it. I also know better what to look for in a partner and what type of person is worth pursuing a sexual and romantic relationship with. I want a partner that pays attention, so I have to pay attention.

I have theorized during my teaching that people develop pop culture obsessions in order to avoid doing something. But I also think it is often that they are looking to learn something, and they find a proper vehicle to teach them. Before I started reading fanfiction every day, I was already trying to change my sex life. I was reading books by sex therapists and trying to find new ways of intimacy in my relationships. But I found that reading self-help books was sterile and not as thrilling as reading about anonymous women's desires and wants on the internet. I still found the information I was looking for - I just found a more exciting way to get it.

I was horribly distracted and missed many deadlines writing this book, but I refused to feel too bad that I got horny for some mind-blowing heterosexual sex while writing about sexual assault. Over the past several years I've had to reclaim my relationships with my body. I now consider my body to be a place of pleasure and not a crime scene.

I want my next story to be not just the lack of sexual assault or abuse, or apathy, but one of a deeply satisfying and happy relationships that coincides with fun, pleasurable sex. One that has many of the elements from fanfiction, words of praise, aftercare, a partner that takes on some of the burden of domestic labor, and a deep sense of trust and love.

In the fanfiction world, when a favorite show ends, writers make up their own stories about what happens next. And for me, a girl whose original story didn't include a happily ever after, that's what fanfiction allows me to do. It shows me that I can figure out what's next and I don't have to worry if it falls within someone else's canon.

The world may tell us the story is over, but all we can do is start writing our own next act.

NEW YEAR, OLD FLAME

On New Year's Eve I woke up to an unexpected Instagram DM.

I recognized the profile bubble-shaped photo before I read the name. Upon recognition, my stomach turned and I said a small prayer that I had not been sleepwalking and messaged him first while I was still dreaming.

It was from Phillip, a man whom I had decided the night before, while sitting alone at the Alamo Drafthouse watching a Christmas season blockbuster, that I was going to stop pining over. Now the worst possible thing was bursting from my phone: hope.

"I never got my review," the message read.

The "review" was for a one-man show of his that I had attended earlier that fall. The show had run successfully on Broadway and then moved onto a theatre in Los Angeles for several months. Puzzled, I stared at my phone as I laid in bed still rubbing the morning crud and previous night's make-up out of my eyes. Why was he sliding into my DMs asking me in the middle of the night what I thought of something I'd seen months ago? As I reread the message it felt, well, flirty.

I met Phillip years previously in Oakland when I was also still performing as a stand-up comedian. I had been embarrassingly late to a show I was booked on due to an Uber Pool that rerouted at least three times and rushed into the venue only to be told the headliner was already on stage and

I'd missed my spot.

I locked eyes with the messy brown-haired boy on stage and felt tingly all over.

"That is the hottest man I have ever seen," I said to the host who was a friend of mine.

"I think he's single," she replied.

"There is no way that man is single," I said, mostly to myself.

A few moments later Phillip jumped off stage, rather ungracefully, and rushed over to introduce himself.

Phillip and I spent that night at the bar in a booth, ignoring the several other people who joined our table. Within ten minutes of sitting down he took out his phone, sitting it next to mine and hitting follow for both of us on each other's profiles as if to say, *we will be keeping in touch after this*. Side by side in our sticky leather booth, we talked about any and all things deep into the night moving through subjects quickly, bouncing from one idea to the next.

I quoted John Waters and he responded with, "Wow, how gay are you?" in a way that made it clear he liked it that I was a little queer and that he was into me, and then proceeded to tell me about the time he made out with a guy in his dorm room at NYU. Then we moved onto comedy and eventually his thoughts on London, where he had just been.

Then rather abruptly, he decided it was time to leave and began asking everyone around if they were heading back across the bridge into San Francisco and if he could catch a ride with them. To my delight, he also ended up taking an Uber Pool, when no one could drive him, making me feel somewhat better about my earlier mishap of missing the show and not like a cheap scumbag.

Still, his departure felt premature; we had been in the middle of a sexy conversation and he didn't seem any less enthusiastic about me as he left, but I couldn't help but feel a little miffed.

Confused and still very smitten, I messaged him later that night about his sudden departure and why the night ended with whiplash instead of a kiss. *Why didn't we kiss?* I asked, choosing the direct approach. Turns out I was right: the hottest man I have ever seen was indeed not single.

But, he assured me in regards to the kiss, *if things were different I would have gotten one.*

What had been a core-shaking romance for me was not just another regular day for the object of my affection.

I tried my best to walk it off. I was living in Portland at the time and he was seemingly bouncing around the entire world. Even if he had felt the same, it wouldn't have worked, I told myself.

So I buried him deep in my *maybe in the future* pile. For the next several years I would see Phillip from time to time at comedy festivals or parties or occasionally when I went out of my way to attend one of his solo shows.

The thing is, I've always been a terrible piner. A hopeless romantic at heart, I do not move on when I feel a connection. I carry a little piece of it with me for years.

For years it felt like we were being pushed together. If I was going to do a run of shows in Seattle, I would check his website and sure enough, he would be in Seattle. If I went to Los Angeles for the weekend, he would be in Los Angeles too. But I was always too nervous to tell him directly that I was still very interested in him. I thought he knew.

When we would see each other we would chat, small talk, but usually we would argue. Never much, but just enough to get me hot. He would tell me I was wrong about something, be it my opinions on a song or the comedian on stage and I would fire back. In retrospect I shouldn't have been attracted to a man who so blatantly disrespected my every opinion, but unfortunately I loved it, wanted nothing more than to push him against a wall and shut him and his incorrect opinions up with my mouth on his. I liked the banter and attention. I liked him. Sometimes I would think of things to say before we met that I knew he would not be able to resist responding to. He always took the bait, much to my delight.

But then without fail, the night would end and I wouldn't see him again for months. Sometimes he didn't even bother to say goodbye to me. I took his distance as a sort of signal. Not yet, this isn't our time.

For my entire life, this has been a habit I have had when I am romantically interested in men. I take their lack of enthusiasm as either a challenge or some secret code only he and I understand.

I will live in what the internet so eloquently calls "delulu land" for far longer than is cute or healthy for me.

But the thing is, dating men is embarrassing. They say dumb things and use you for your labor, and you find yourself having less than satisfying sex with them. Pining over a man, however, is thrilling! It involves long glances across crowded parties and bus rides in the rain to comedy festivals so I can catch one glimpse of the object of my affection. I loved pining over Phillip, he was easy to yearn for and always on the move and out of reach.

Eventually I started living with a serious boyfriend I had acquired (whom I did not enjoy arguing with and did not find intellectually stimulating) and then slowly stopped pursuing comedy as I focused more on writing books. After COVID lockdown ended, I realized it had been years since Phillip and I had been in the same room, but he was always in the back of my mind and I always harbored a small bit of hope that he would come back into my life.

After moving to California and having dumped my boring boyfriend, I saw an advertisement for Phillip's one-man show's several monthlong residency in my Gmail. Roughly five years since our first meeting, we were both living in Los Angeles and if the grapevine was correct, both single. I was already imagining our late dinners at Little Doms followed by a healthy amount of arguing over new releases at Skylight. I wanted to stare into his beautiful blue eyes while I told him his opinions on Bret Easton Ellis sounded like he got them from a Reddit thread.

That led me to his show that fall, after which I hung back in hopes of reconnecting, but I wasn't able to catch him. It did lead to months of resurfaced pining and daydreaming about sitting on his face so he couldn't say something dumb to me with his perfect mouth.

Now here it was - New Year's Eve - and I got a message from the guy I could never really forget. Didn't he know New Year's was the start of nearly every good rom-com?

New Year's also known as when Bridget Jones meets Mark Darcy, or when Harry and Sally finally get together, or when we finally get to see Cameron Diaz and Kate Winslet have their happy ever afters in *The Holiday*. New Year's Eve is the day when unrequited love becomes requited, the day when everything starts or ends. Or both.

Messaging a woman on New Year's Eve? Definitely one hundred percent a flirt, I thought to myself.

We exchanged some very much less flirty messages before Phillip left me on "read" and I doubled-messaged him to scold him for messaging me on New Year's Eve when he knew I had a thing for him "for like ever."

He assured me he had no idea I was into him. I wasn't sure I believed him, but at least now he knew. Maybe something would happen now.

For the next few months, I was overwhelmed after releasing my first book and Phillip was busy having the most successful year of his career so I didn't immediately lose hope when nothing happened after our holiday exchange.

Unfortunately one little message had unlocked a wave of feelings and emotions I had up to that point kept dormant. Now that the floodgates were open, I was in peak pining mode where, despite being a woman with a book to promote, he consumed a not insignificant amount of my brain space.

"Well, he's definitely thinking about you, something is marinating inside there," my friend Laura offered as I laid on her couch in Eagle Rock relaying my tale of woe while I wolfed down a plate of Leo's Tacos.

A few months later, I went to another one of Phillip's comedy shows with a few friends. This time waiting around to speak with him after. We chatted briefly outside a theatre in downtown Los Angeles while managing to make my friends very uncomfortable with the sparky tension that can only come from five years of build-up.

"Oh man, someone has a crush on you," my friend Greg teased me as we drove home on the 101.

"When am I going to hear from him?" I asked, my heart beating with anticipation.

""'Oh, definitely probably tonight, if not tomorrow," Greg offered.

I never did hear from him. When I attempted to engage with him on Instagram, I never got more than the occasional short response of politeness.

One day, in the midst of my pining, I listened to a podcast while he was a guest. The host asked him to describe what he was looking for in a romantic partner and he said he was looking for "a beautiful and hilarious writer girlfriend."

I wanted to scream, and do some other things, but I chose to avoid any actions that would lead to a conviction for first degree manslaughter. Instead I replied to one of his Instagram stories with a fire emoji. Then a few more with some of my best funny responses that he would heart but not respond to.

Eventually, he stopped responding to me altogether.

Our longest correspondence had been the one on New Year's Eve. Turns out it was not the beginning of our rom-com that I had hoped for. I once again had to come to terms with what felt like sparks all around for me, was not the same on the other end. I immediately fell into an unrequited love-induced slump Bridget Jones or Kate Winslet would understand as I tried not to feel a little led-on.

I moped around my apartment, complained to all my friends, and read a lot of Henry Miller while I drank entire pots of coffee in one sitting. I tried to romanticize my pain, thinking that if my unrequited love slowly killed me it would be worth it. That only lasted about a week and then I was bored.

Unfortunately, the pining was no longer thrilling because the breadcrumbs were gone. Now all I was left with was the reality that I had a six year situationship with a man who fed me the bare minimum to keep my attention and thought my taste in pretty much everything warranted a squabble.

At least it could have been worse, I told myself, I could have actually had to seriously date him, that would have been a bloodbath.

Perhaps a relationship where you expect the other person to always be combative with you, isn't the fairy tale an adult woman of considerable talent and beauty such as myself should be hoping for.

In the middle of what felt like a tortuous year of bereftness, Phillip was promoting his first ever television special. I was desperately trying not to allow a man whose eyes are too close together, but whom I adored anyway, to consume my every thought, but unfortunately he seemed to be everywhere.

The promotion included a billboard on Sunset Boulevard across from the Comedy Store, or right smack in the middle of my daily commute to my day job in Westwood.

Every day I would have to wake up and drive past the man I was desperately trying to forget. I would stare at his face and try to remind myself that I deserved better than someone who left me on "read" or gave me one word answers or tried to fight with me because he didn't think drag queens could be funny.

I tried to alter my commute, but Santa Monica had much more traffic and any side street always had some type of obstacle that would cause me to be late. It was my best bet to keep an extra ten minutes of sleep.

What had previously felt like a normal commute, now felt long and torturous. I have never been more aware of LA traffic as I occasionally spent thirty-five minutes with his picture in front of me and no way to quickly drive away.

"LA is the only city that will do that to you, it will take someone who you feel has wronged you and put them on a billboard so you can't escape," Laura offered in sympathy.

In many of my favorite rom-coms, the leads learn their lesson on New Year's. The loop ends, the credits roll. They say that the universe will keep sending you the same message until you learn. If you don't get the message the first time, it will come back again until you do.

Sometimes it even puts the lesson on a billboard, so you can't miss it.

HELP ME STEP THROUGH THE GLASS DOROTHY

In the spring of 2025 I went on a date with a woman I met on Hinge. Kath and I met at a taco bar in Silverlake, Los Angeles's most lesbian neighborhood, and shared appetizers while sipping overpriced mocktails. We talked about film editing, her next and my upcoming first trip to Europe, and how we balanced our day jobs with our artistic careers.

She was the first masculine-presenting woman I'd been on a date with. I found her charming and thought her gorgeous smile was an alluring mix of both pretty and handsome. Despite her being over a decade older than me, the conversation flowed naturally, and we seemed to have a lot in common. She was more attractive in person than her photos, and she only intimidated me enough to make me hornier rather than nervous. Overall, I was having a pretty great time.

A little over an hour into the date, we ordered some desserts to share and as I slid my spoon into our strawberry tres leches cake, I noticed her face turned serious.

"So, how long have you been dating women?" Kath asked me.

Slightly freaked out, I started on a long, jumbled mess of answers and babbled about how I have never really dated a woman.

Kissed? Yes.

Pined for? Yes.

Been in love with? Yes.

But dated? Technically no.

Kath smiled politely and proceeded to tell me a little bit about her own dating history, a series of medium-term relationships, many with women for whom she was their first lesbian partner.

"I only date people who have had at least two prior relationships with women," Kath said with a tone that could only be read as *this case is now closed.*

She was smiling at me politely but my spine now felt tingly, as if cold water had been poured down my back.

Before I could respond to what felt like a rather harsh rejection, she continued, "I have dated too many people who are in some type of transition process in their lives. I never know if they really like me or if they like the new experience. I always have to guide them through it. Not only intimacy, but other things, like telling their families they are dating a woman or being seen in public on a date with a woman."

I wanted to interject that I had been out to most of my family since my early twenties or high school and that I was, in fact, in public and on a date with a woman at that moment. Instead I felt embarrassed and out of my league.

Now in my thirties, I feel extremely comfortable in my queerness. It is a part of me larger than my breath itself. My queerness is as essential to my being as the blood that flows through my veins. Every thought that passes in between my ears is informed by it. I have, however, felt extremely uncomfortable when it comes to acting on that queerness in the form of intimacy. In that, I have never really had a real adult relationship with another woman.

In some way I feel stunted. Being queer can feel like an

endless adolescence.

As a child, my favorite movie to rent at both the Hollywood Video in Lebanon, Oregon (my father's video rental store), and at the Video Circle in Philomath, Oregon (my grandmother's video rental store), was *Return to Oz*.[*] As a child who bounded around multiple homes, one thing I knew for sure was that I could get multiple adults to rent the VHS tape for me so I could at least see it a few times a year, even if one of them said "no" or "you've already seen that."

Return to Oz, is technically the 1995 sequel to *The Wonderful Wizard of Oz*. Despite being a Disney movie, I would more describe it as a horror movie for children who are about to find out they are part of the LGBTQ community. The movie has been considered to be an awakening for so many of my fellow queers that I frequently bring it up at gay bars if I feel like the conversation needs a little help.

Return to Oz starts with Dorothy, back in Kansas after her adventures in the first movie, only nobody believes her stories of the magical land of Oz and the friends she's made there. Thinking she is having hallucinations and going mad, Auntie Em takes Dorothy to a mental institution where an evil doctor and his equally evil nurse plan to perform electroshock therapy on her. Electroshock therapy, famously also used on gay and lesbians as a form of conversion therapy, evokes a frightening parallel of what can happen to a young person who lives their truth.

While first looking at the electroshock machine, that's supposed to cure her of her "dreams," Dorthoty sees a

[*] I am sure at one point I also got my mother to rent *Return to Oz* at the Corvallis Hollywood Video.

reflection in its glass, only it is not her own, but another girl with long blonde hair who appears in the mirror behind her.

Auntie Em leaves Dorothy for treatment at the institution and she is then strapped to a table so the shock therapy can begin. Luckily our blonde heroine returns and rescues Dorothy while the evil nurse is distracted by a power outage caused by a storm. Neither Dorothy nor the audience know who this little girl is, but we both immediately feel a kinship with her; she speaks to Dorothy with immediate familiarity. To the viewer, Dorothy and the unnamed girl appear to be some sort of supernatural twins or perhaps the other half of the same whole. Two girls of about the same age, one with blonde tresses and the other with brunette braids. Although it is never explicitly declared, it is clear the other girl is inflicted with the same disease as Dorothy: as in, she also knows about Oz.

As Dorothy's blonde twin and savior unstraps her from the table, she explains that the machine damages patients (I agree - turning straight would be very damaging). They escape the mental institution, attempting to evade the evil nurse who chases after them by crossing a roaring river. Due to the stormy weather and the river's rough conditions, Dorothy is separated from her counterpart mid-escape and floats away on a chicken coop. When she awakes, she is back in the Land of Oz, along with her chicken Belina who has miraculously joined her.

The identity of Dorothy's blonde twin is not revealed until the end of the film, but she is Ozma, the true princess of Oz. Or to me at the time of my childhood viewing, the most beautiful girl I ever saw. My first girl crush. When I watched the film, after convincing whatever adult I could manipulate into renting it for me again, I greedily waited for glimpses of Ozma. I wanted to be her - blonde, assured, and beautiful - but I also wanted to be Dorothy so I could talk to her, be rescued by her, and hold her delicate hand in mine. I never wanted to be rescued by a handsome prince, but I dreamed of the regal and slightly taller Ozma appearing out of nowhere to whisk me to a land of magic, friendship, and safety.

Unfortunately, the Land of Oz that Dorothy returns to is one in severe distress. Dorothy finds the Scarecrow (who was appointed to rule over the Emerald City by the Wizard) has been replaced by the evil Princess Mombi and all the residences of the Emerald City have been turned to stone. I don't believe the creators of a 1995 Disney film intended to make a metaphor about the decline of queer spaces and community, but I will say as I watched the film recently that the ruby encrusted shoe sure did fit.

Horrified but determined to help the land she loves, Dorothy (along with her chicken) quickly finds a new chosen family of misfits. Before his capture, the Scarecrow left Tik-Tok "The Royal Army of Oz," to wait for Dorothy and assist her in overthrowing Mombi. Tik-Tok is a mechanical man, who has separate clockwork springs for thinking, walking and speaking. In Mombi's residence Dorothy also finds Jack Pumpkinhead, a man with a straw body and smiling jack-o'-lantern for a head. Upon their meeting, Jack remarks that Dorothy looks like his mother, who created him with magic life power, and asks if he can call her mom too. His mother is later revealed to be Ozma.*

* I believe Jack then refers to both of them as mom as he is now the son of lesbians.

Ozma, on the other hand, is nowhere to be found, but she appears to Dorothy in the mirrors throughout Oz giving Dorothy clues and subtle directions.[1]

~

I don't think I found my footing as a "practicing queer" until I moved to LA. My own Emerald City. Before that I was more of a cultural queer, who only spent a few hours making out with women on the big holidays like Christmas and Easter. When I lived in Portland, I had many queer friends and spent plenty of time in gay bars, but I felt too close to a version of myself, the Kansas version of myself, to really let go and let myself be rescued by a beautiful tall blonde. Once I was in Los Angeles, I could find my own Ozmas and Tik-Toks and chosen family without worrying if someone was going to see me on a date and tattle on me to my mother who would not judge but would probably ask a question I wasn't ready to answer.

Sometimes when you are figuring it out, what can be perceived as a prying eye is enough to keep you from going further. I honestly cannot tell you if I have a problem or if my family is as bad with boundaries as I think they are, but I often feel they ask me too many invasive questions about who I date and what that person is like and provide too many opinions on it. Either way, I have never felt like I was able to date truly alone.

In truth, I have never been great at romantic intimacy. I feel uncomfortable being perceived as half of a relationship even if I like my partner. I have nightmares where someone I know runs into me on a date. I am even worse when it comes to dating women, who usually have the emotional intelligence to sense my discomfort and feel when I am hiding from them. I also felt insecure in how much of a rush I felt when dating a woman, not wanting to put so many emotions and inexperience on someone else. I needed an Oz, a place where I could find love and intimacy first, and *then* figure out how to bring it into the rest of my life. A place where I could be free before bringing my date home to Kansas.

Once in Los Angeles, where queers have come so they could finally be themselves since the city's inception, I no longer worried about the opinions of anyone back home. I started a reading series at a lesbian bar. I hit on women. I asked women for kisses at gay bars. I got kisses from women at gay bars. I changed my Hinge preferences. I finally felt calm.

With her new chosen family, Dorothy attempts to rescue her best friend the Scarecrow, who we find out has been captured by Princess Mombi's father the Nome King. They travel to the Nome King's mountain to ask him to free the Scarecrow. It is also revealed to the audience that Mombi has trapped Ozma in the mirrors within the Royal Palace of Oz.

My bisexuality can sometimes feel like a mirror. On one hand when I see my reflection there is my straight self, but there is also something else, another part of me behind glass but visible to those who are in the know.

I loved the movie *Return to Oz* so much as a kid that I started reading L. Frank Baum's *Oz* books. I was able to spend more time with Dorothy and the Scarecrow in their special land filled with beings the author refers to as "queers."

"You have some queer friends, Dorothy," the fairy

Polychrome remarks in *The Road to Oz*.

To which Dorothy replies. "The queerness doesn't matter, so long as they're friends"[2]

For me, the most comforting part of the Oz books has always been the depiction of these queer bodies. Almost all the residents of Oz live within bodies that look or act like men, but are not quite human beings. L. Frank Baum referred to them as "queerly made men" specifically referencing the Scarecrow and Tin Man.[3] In *Return to Oz*, Jack Pumpkinhead and Tik-Tok are arguably also queerly made men, with bodies of straw and metal. These "queerly made" beings may live among regular men, but their bodies are different. They are queer bodies.

I also know what it's like to live in a queerly made body. I often feel like my body has switches like Tik-Tok's and I am on permanent "frolic mode," unable to control my arms and legs as easily as a regular human woman who can walk through the world with grace and poise. I am like Scarecrow blowing in the wind or, like Jack, I am constantly checking my head for soft spots or, like Tin Man, I can rust over if not oiled properly. My body may look like it was meant for this world, but its operating system says otherwise.

Whether the author intended it or not, these metaphors are so recognized by the queer community that "Friend of Dorothy" became slang for gay men and used throughout the twentieth century.

It is also believed Scarecrow and Tin Man were famously hinted to be lovers.[*]

---

[*] It is because of this relationship I will never be able to be a *Wicked* fan.

There lived in the Land of Oz two queerly made men who were the best of friends. They were so much happier when together that they were seldom apart; yet they liked to separate, once in a while, that they might enjoy the pleasure of meeting again.[4]

As a kid reading the books, I did not understand the subtext but was intrigued by the intimacy in their friendship. In *The Marvelous Land of Oz*, Scarecrow declares that they have decided to never be parted from each other. In the Tin Woodsman's house, the Scarecrow's portrait hangs above the mantle. I cataloged these tiny moments between them, the details of their relationship made me feel tingly.

Interestingly, the Ozma of the books is considered the first trans character in literature. As a child, Princess Mombi turns her into a boy named Tip in order to prevent her from claiming their rightful throne. Tip lives as a boy with no memory of being Ozma until Glinda the Good Witch discovers what happened and transforms Tip back into a princess with the appearance of a fourteen-year-old girl.

Ozma and Dorothy as lovers is similarly hinted at in the original canon. When Ozma reigns as queen, Dorothy is the only person allowed to enter the royal bedchambers unannounced. Ozma makes Dorothy a princess and they share many, although platonic on paper, goodbye kisses throughout the series. Most notably and romantic to me is that Ozma in both *Return to Oz* and the book's canon promises to look out for Dorothy and notes that if she sees any sign she either misses Oz or is in trouble, she will send for her right away.

A fair question I get asked by concerned, and usually straight, friends is why I don't simply go out and date a bunch of women. Like queerness is a game that has to be won.

That bisexuality has to be proved through numbers. But I have never approached intimacy or relationships in that way. Despite this, in moments of insecurity I sometimes feel like I should have started aggressively dating women sooner. Like I have to get out there and force experiences in order to be real. But I am not an aggressive dater in general for any gender. I prefer to wait and see who I meet on my journey. Someone will always come out of the woods if you keep walking down the yellow brick road.

In the end of *Return to Oz*, Dorothy defeats the Nome King, captures Princess Mobi, and rescues the Scarecrow. Back in the Emerald City, the residents of Oz are brought back to life, freed from their stone figures, and a huge celebration commences at the Royal Palace. Now with a restored Oz, the residents of the Emerald City party and honor Dorothy, asking her to become their queen. Dorothy apologizes for she wishes to return to Kansas, but in that moment Ozma appears in the mirror.

"It's you," Dorothy proclaims as she approaches Ozma, delighted to see her after she assumed she had drowned in the river.

Ozma asks Dorothy to help her to step through the glass. Dorothy seems hesitant at first, unsure how to grant the request, but cautiously moves her hand to the flat surface and the two girls' fingers entwine as Dorothy chivalrously helps Ozma out of the mirror. As Ozma steps out, Dorothy immediately tells her how beautiful she is.

"Help me step through the glass, Dorothy."

"You're sooooo beautiful."[5]

I sometimes still find myself repeating these lines from

what I consider to be a very romantic moment in cinema and I switch roles constantly, wanting to be both Dorothy and Ozma simultaneously. In their relationship, both girls get a chance to be both rescuee and rescuer. I wanted to be loved by the beautiful Ozma, but also I wanted a Dorothy, someone to pull me onto the other side.

I feel like I exist in the space of being both a queer elder and a baby gay. My status as queer eldership comes from the amount of time I have spent in queer spaces, part of queer communities, and participating in deeply fulfilling but not always sexual queer relationships. I've protested, marched, as well as participated in other forms of activism. I've built a close-knit chosen family, dropped off friends at the bathhouse, and buried others in the morning. I've been a part of this community for decades, and then sometimes I see a pretty girl from across the street and I clam up and feel like I did in high school.

In truth I have had many Dorothys in my life. Queer women of all kinds who have slowly pulled me out of my mirrored prison and onto dance floors or into their arms. Because I was never in the closet, I was always in a mirror. I can see out and they can see me.

At the restaurant Kath and I continued to talk about our relationship history. Because it was a lesbian date, even after she rejected me we had to process it for another hour before we could legally leave the restaurant. Rosie O'Donnell can send you a citation in the mail if you don't abide by these rules.

I left Kath for a moment to pay my part of the bill at the bar. While I waited for the bartender's attention, I noticed a handsome man next to me sitting by himself and swiping on Hinge. Choosing to not feel defeated and to be proud of bisexuality, I thought about asking him for his number. The bartender approached me and before I could ask to close out my tab, the handsome man interrupted.

"Hey man, who can I reach out to here about booking, I'm a DJ? "

I quickly paid my tab and accepted that the evening was just going to have to be a dud.

Outside Kath and I hugged and exchanged "nice meeting yous" knowing we would never see each other again.

She was not my Dorothy and that's okay. Because I am a queer type stuck in an unruly body, I will simply hang out on the side of the yellow brick road and wait. I hope eventually she will come skipping towards me.

In Kansas, nobody believes Dorothy has been to Oz. They don't see the magic. They may think she is just a normal girl, but Dorothy is part of Oz. She lived there, her friends are there, and it's where she became who she's meant to be even if everyone back in Kansas can't see it. I remind myself of this if someone questions my queerness, which to be honest hasn't happened in years. To some, I read very straight, but the Tik-Toks, Pumpkinheads, and Ozmas meant for me, have never had trouble identifying me as a fellow resident of Oz. They know I'm "a friend of Dorothy."

As I write this, I'm planning another date with a woman. I asked her out after sliding in the DMs because I found her interesting. She's funny, has strawberry blonde hair, and hosts a podcast. I'm intrigued, but not smitten. I'm not falling head over heels pining over her. It's mundane, which is what I wanted it to be. Comfort can be kinda boring, but at this point in my life, I want peace.

Oz knows peace when Ozma is in charge, when it is no longer ruled by the Wizard's theatrics or Mombi's chaos. When she is finally on the right side of the glass.

NOTES

Introduction: On Parody

[1] "Better Legal Research | Casetext," n.d., https://web.archive.org/web/20190502112119/https://casetext.com/.

[2] Aqua. Barbie Girl. Universal, MCA Records, 1997.

[3] Sanford, Arlene, director. *A Very Brady Sequel*. Paramount Pictures, 1996. 1hr., 29 min.

[4] Roan, Chappell. Pink Pony Club. Atlantic Records, 2020.

Because My Mom Can't Cry

[1] Ephron, Nora, director. *This is My Life*. 20th Century Fox, 1992. 1 hr., 45 min.

Note: The film Heart and Souls *is discussed throughout this essay, but not directly cited:*

Underwood, Ron, director. *Heart and Souls*. Universal Pictures, 1993. 1 hr., 44 min.

Fighting for Kathleen

[1] Bikini Kill, Rebel Girl. Kill Rock Stars, 1993.

[2] Anderson, Sini, director. *The Punk Singer*. Sundance Selects, 2013. 1 hr., 20 min.

[3] HARDTIMES, "Hot Tips to Get You Bikini Kill Ready This Summer," June 12, 2016, https://thehardtimes.net/news/hot-tips-get-bikini-kill-ready-summer/.

What To Wear to Meet Your Hero

[1] Waters, John, director. *Female Trouble*. New Line Cinema,

1974. 1 hr., 37 min. (original).

Note: This essay also makes references, without direct citation, to the following titles:
- Shankman, Adam, director. *Hairspray*. New Line Cinema (US), 2007. 1 hr., 56 min.
- Waters, John, director. *Cry-Baby*. Universal Pictures, 1990. 1 hr., 25 min.
- Waters, John, director. *Female Trouble*. New Line Cinema, 1974. 1 hr., 37 min. (original).
- Waters, John, director. *Hairspray*. New Line Cinema, 1988. 1 hr., 32 min.
- Waters, John, director. *Pecker*. Fine Line Features, 1998. 1 hr., 26 min.
- Waters, John, director. *Pink Flamingos*. New Line Cinema, 1972. 1 hr., 32 min.
- Waters, John, director. *Polyester*. New Line Cinema, 1981. 1 hr., 26 min.

Big Daddy's Little Lady

Note: The Golden Girls *episode, "Big Daddy's Little Lady" is referenced and directly cited throughout this essay, as indicated by the footnote below.*

[1] *The Golden Girls*, season 2 episode 6, "Big Daddy's Little Lady," directed by Russell Marcus, aired November 15th, 1986, on NBC.

Before We Said #MeToo

[1] Bowley, Graham, Sydney Ember, Matt Stevens, Lauren McCarthy, and Maira Garcia. 2021. "Bill Cosby: Actor

Freed after Sexual Assault Conviction Is Overturned." *The New York Times*, June 30, 2021. https://www.nytimes.com/live/2021/06/30/arts/bill-cosby-released.

[2,3] "Louis C.K.'S Full Statement." 2017. CNN. November 10, 2017. https://www.cnn.com/2017/11/10/entertainment/louis-ck-full-statement.

[4,5] Scott, Ridley, director. *Thelma & Louise*. MGM-Pathé Communications, 1991. 2 hr., 9 min.

[6] Ferrara, Abel, director. *Ms .45*. Rochelle Films (United States), Warner Bros. Pictures (international), 1981. 1 hr., 20 min.

What Fran Wore

[1] Fran Fine Fashion (@WhatFranWore), Instagram, https://www.instagram.com/whatfranwore/

[2] *The Nanny*, season 3, episode 15, "Fashion Show," directed by Dorothy Lyman, aired January 8, 1996, on CBS.

Marc Jacobs Perfectly Imperfect

[1] Jeena Sharma, "You Could Be the Face of Marc Jacobs' Next Campaign," *PAPER Magazine*, June 15, 2020, https://www.papermag.com/marc-jacobs-campaign-fragrance#rebelltitem4.

[2] Caroline Leaper, "16 Marc Jacobs Quotes That Prove He Is the Wisest of Fashion Gods," *Marie Claire UK*, April 9, 2015, https://www.marieclaire.co.uk/news/fashion-news/marc-jacobs-quotes-93286.

Final Girl

[1] Strauss-Schulson, Todd, director. *The Final Girls*. Stage 6 Films, 2015. 1 hr., 31 min.

[2] T. Rex. 20th Century Boy. T. REX (UK), Ariola (Germany), 1973.

[3] Rossi, Carla. 2026. "Anthony Hudson / Carla Rossi." Anthony Hudson / Carla Rossi. 2026. https://www.thecarlarossi.com/why.

[4] Wikipedia Contributors. 2019. "Final Girl." Wikipedia. Wikimedia Foundation. September 8, 2019. https://en.wikipedia.org/wiki/Final_girl.

[5, 6] Clover, Carol J. *Men, Women, and Chain Saws: Gender in the Modern Horror Film*. Princeton University Press, 1992.

I Can't Say Moschino

[1] Sirera, Lindsey. 2015. "Bitch Stole My Look! Rihanna & Kesha Rock the Same 'You Will Never Own Me' Dress." E! Online. E! News. June 2, 2015. https://www.eonline.com/news/662325/bitch-stole-my-look-rihanna-kesha-rock-the-same-you-will-never-own-me-dress.

[2] Brantley, Ben. 1990. "DESIGNING ANARCHIST." Vanity Fair | the Complete Archive. Vanity Fair. March 1990. https://vanityfair.azurewebsites.net/article/1990/03/01/designing-anarchist.

[3,5] *The Simpsons*, season 7, episode 14, "Scenes from the Class Struggle in Springfield," directed by Susie Dietter, aired February 4, 1996, on FOX.

[4] "Franco Moschino." n.d. British Vogue. https://www.vogue.co.uk/gallery/franco-moschino-talks-to-gq.

Carrie's Credit Cards

[1] *Sex and the City*, season 2, episode 16, "Was It Good for You?," directed by Dan Algrant, aired September 19, 1999, on HBO.

[2,7] *Sex and the City*, season 4, episode 16, "Ring a Ding Ding," directed by Alan Taylor, aired January 27, 2002, on HBO.

[3] Jackson, Jame. 2018. "Carrie Bradshaw Has $1 Million Worth of Debt and Now I Feel Better about My Spending Habits." BuzzFeed. June 27, 2018. https://www.buzzfeed.com/jamedjackson/carrie-bradshaw-has-1-million-worth-of-debt-and-now-i-feel.

[4,5] ELLE. 2021. "The Irony of Writers Who Dress Well," August 2, 2021. https://www.elle.com/fashion/personal-style/a37170265/writers-who-dress-well-essay/.

[6] *Sex and the City*, season 6, episode 1, "To Market, to Market," directed by Michael Patrick King, aired June 22, 2003, on HBO.

[8] Staples, L. (2022, January 28). *When Did Carrie Bradshaw Get So Rich?* The Cut. https://www.thecut.com/2022/01/and-just-like-that-money-carrie-rich.html

I Want a Man with a Slutty Neck

[1] *Bridgerton*, season 1, episode 1, "Diamond of the First Water," directed by Julie Anne Robinson, aired December 25, 2020, on Netflix.

[2] Nathanson, Hannah. 2026. "'I'm Really Sensitive with People I Care About.' Nicola Coughlan Stands Her Ground." ELLE. March 5, 2026. https://www.elle.com/uk/life-and-culture/a70585011/nicola-coughlan/.

[3] Dworkin, Andrea. *Pornography: Men Possessing Women.* Plume,

1981.

⁴ Erika Lust, "It's Time for Porn to Change," TEDx Talks, Vienna, Austria, November 2014, 12 min., 55 sec., https://youtu.be/Z9LaQtfpP_8?si=E40mCDVsnGqWghhX

⁵ *Bridgerton*, season 3, episode 4, "Old Friends" directed by Andrew Ahn, aired May 16, 2024, on Netflix.

⁶ *Bridgerton*, season 1, episode 6, "Swish," directed by Julie Anne Robinson, aired December 25, 2020, on Netflix.

⁷ Quinn, Julia. *Romancing Mister Bridgerton*. Avon, 2002.

⁸ for, Organization. 2024. "It's about Being Safe, Trusted and Loved… || Polin Kinktober - MoirinDC - Bridgerton (TV) [Archive of Our Own]." Archiveofourown.org. 2024. https://archiveofourown.org/series/4408171.

⁹ Sehgal, Parul. 2021. "The Case against the Trauma Plot." The New Yorker. December 23, 2021. https://www.newyorker.com/magazine/2022/01/03/the-case-against-the-trauma-plot.

¹⁰ "BOMB Magazine | Jamie Hood by Elizabeth Teets." 2025. BOMB Magazine. 2025. https://bombmagazine.org/articles/2025/02/04/jamie-hood-by-elizabeth-teets/.

Help Me Step Through the Glass Dorothy

^{1, 5} Murch, Walter, director. *Return to Oz*. Buena Vista Distribution Co. (United States); Walt Disney Productions (UK), 1985. 1 hr., 53 min.

² Baum, L. Frank. *The Road to Oz*. Reilly & Britton, 1909.

^{3, 4} Baum, L Frank. 2026. "The Scarecrow and the Tin Woodman." American Literature. 2026. https://americanliterature.com/author/l-frank-baum/short-story/the-scarecrow-and-the-tin-woodman.

ACKNOWLEDGMENTS

First and foremost I want to thank my dear friend Samantha Mann for being my champion, without her I don't think I would be anything besides a girl in a cool coat who thinks about writing books. I cannot thank you enough for being this book's doula and fairy godmother.

Very early drafts of this book were created in Chloe Caldwell's one year essay generator class and without her beyond marvelous mentorship as well as the time, care, and attention of my classmates, I would not be carrying around copies of this book in my Versace purse today. I also want to thank that one girl for being an absolute hater, enemies are the spice of life and wow, did you make things flavorful.

Thank you to my best friends and inspirations, Greg, Megan, and Ella. Thank you to Anthony and Pepper for being both major influences on this book but also on me. Thank you for knowing me, thank you for loving me. Thanks to tall handsome Brandon, even though he did not come over to eat Beef Wellington with me in bed during the writing of this book and I'm still mad about it.

Thank you Tomy, I love you.

To the team at Read Furiously for their expertise and patience, and Samantha Atzeni for championing this book.

And as always, thank you Mommy. May our lives be tangled up together for always.

ABOUT THE AUTHOR

Elizabeth Teets is an Oregon born writer, comedian, screenwriter, and fashionista. Her work has appeared in *Los Angeles Times*, *New York Times*, *Interview Magazine*, *Catapult*, *Reductress*, and more. She lives in Los Angeles where she is waiting for her group chat to respond.

Find Elizabeth online at:
elizabethteets.com
instagram.com/elteets

MORE FROM ELIZABETH TEETS

"I love this witty, heartfelt, thoughtful book that pays homage to my very favorite genre: movies about women.

- Kirsten "Kiwi" Smith, co-screenwriter of *Legally Blonde, 10 Things I Hate About You, She's the Man*

Elizabeth Teet's "Isn't She Great" is the anthology book I didn't know I needed.

- Laurie Kilmartin, Longtime CONAN writer, author of *Dead People Suck*

Learn more at **readfuriously.com/elizabeth-teets**

A Note to our Furious Readers

From all of us at Read Furiously, we hope you enjoyed *I Blame Television: Essays on the Pop Culture that Raised, Ruined, and Enraptured Me.*

We pledge to donate a portion of these book sales to causes that are special to Read Furiously. These causes are chosen with the intent to better the lives of others who are struggling to tell their own stories.

Reading is more than a passive activity – it is the opportunity to play an active role within our world. Each cause has been researched thoroughly, discussed openly, and voted upon carefully by our team of Read Furiously editors.

To find out more about who, what, why, and where Read Furiously lends its support, please visit our website at readfuriously.com/charity

Read Often, Read Well,
Read Furiously!